Praise for
Important Catholic Women of the 20th Century: Stories of Courage and Fear, Unassuming Audacity and Everyday Drudgery, Connected by Faith

"This is an informative book of Catholic women activists, poets, saints and nuns, with historical facts at the beginning, and thought-provoking questions for introspection or discussions at the end of each chapter. It is the kind of book that would be lovely to see on the bookshelves of homes, libraries and faith retreats. It is well-written and documented, with relevant websites and sources provided in its references section."

- 2025 Catholic Media Association Book Awards

I0152845

ALSO BY LOREL WILHELM-VOLPI

An I Love You Book for People About to Take on the World

An I Love You Calendar for People About to Take on the World

Important Catholic Women of the 20th Century

Stories of Courage and Fear, Unassuming Audacity and Everyday Drudgery, Connected by Faith

Lorel Wilhelm-Volpi

VELMA

LITTLE ROCK

Velma

Published by Velma

815 Technology Dr, #241193, Little Rock, AR 72223

© Copyright 2024 by Lorel Wilhelm-Volpi

Print ISBN: 979-8-9919419-0-7

eBook ISBN: 979-8-9919419-1-4

Cover design and illustration: Bryan Arendt

Acknowledgments

I could not have even begun to bring this project to life without the support of my husband, Angelo Volpi - the best sounding board on the planet. I love you more than words can say.

Before I was ready to share this widely, I gave early drafts to Stefana Hungary, Shelby Koons and Michela Palmieri. Their feedback and ideas have made this a much better book. I am so grateful to each of you for sharing your time and energy with me- I cannot thank you enough!

Last but not least, every day my family inspires me to be a better person (try to anyway!). Thank you, Angelo, Victoria, Matteo and Elisabeth, for keeping me on my toes and for your love. I love you more!

Table of Contents

How to Use This Book

Each chapter features a brief biography of a different Catholic woman from the 20th century. To help place their incredible stories in the proper context, the chapters start with a brief historical snapshot of significant events and societal movements. And because the common thread among these stories is the shared Catholic faith of these women, the book begins with a brief overview of major events and themes in the life of the Roman Catholic Church in the past century.

The goal of this volume, and the selection of the women's stories herein, is to offer a sampling of strong, faithful women who we might look to for inspiration or intercession. Reflection questions are included at the end of the chapter to help you explore some of the lessons each woman's life may offer and what they might mean for you.

Introduction

Saint Joan of Arc's famous words, "I am not afraid for God is with me. I was born for this!" have resonated through the centuries for good reason. She calls us to boldness—to a willingness to embrace our current moment and share the Gospel without fear, no matter what circumstances lie before us.

On the surface, it's easy to assume boldness means doing things the Joan of Arc way: riding into battle or confronting a wayward king. But boldness doesn't always mean taking actions that change the course of the type of history written about in textbooks. It can take the form of subtle actions that, at the time, might not even be noticed—let alone thought of as something bold.

Boldness can mean clinging to your convictions in the face of familial disapproval, financial hardship, societal ridicule, and prejudice from friends and neighbors. Sometimes, boldness can be as simple as publicly declaring, "I am Catholic," in a situation where the reaction might be less than positive. The stories in these pages showcase women whose boldness echoes in diverse ways.

Some of them were mothers, while others were single or members of religious life. They lived in different countries on different continents. But what they had in common was that they all boldly lived their faith and brought the light of Christ to the people around them. They were unafraid to embrace who God had called them to be.

This may or may not be a book about saints, although some of the women chronicled here are saints, some are formally on the path to sainthood, and some may one day be recognized as saints. This is, first and foremost, a book about ordinary women who lived their lives in extraordinary ways as they served God and others. They're incredibly relatable to women of all ages and stages in life.

In these pages, you'll read about women who were drawn to a traditional vocation as wives and mothers. You'll read about women who lived out their call to consecrated religious life. And you'll read about women whose vocation was to live a single life. Their daily responsibilities may have looked different, but they all shared one thing: They were dedicated to following God's will.

For some of these women, God led them to a life of activism and promoting social justice, whether on behalf of workers' rights or standing up for those facing racial or ethnic discrimination. Others followed God's call to a life of service to the poor. Some balanced being a working professional with raising their children. Their different paths highlight the diversity of women's roles in the Church and the varied ways that women can make a difference in the world.

Women like Dorothy Day and Sofía del Valle vocally stood up for social justice and used their position as laywomen to bring Catholic social teachings to the cultures around them. Other women, like Mother Teresa and Sr. Irmã Dulce Lopes Pontes, answered a calling to religious life and then ministered to the poor, making sure every person they encountered knew that God loved them. Women like Margit Slachta and Cory Aquino entered the political sphere to fight for human dignity, while women like Thea Bowman and Boleslawa Lament served marginalized communities and worked toward cultural unity.

Women like Margarete Sommer and Gertrud Luckner were witnesses to the Catholic faith amidst the horrors of the Holocaust, while women like Anuarite Nengapeta and Daphrose Rugamba became martyrs for their faith. And women like Gianna Beretta Molla and Maria Quattrocchi demonstrated the sanctifying power of marriage and family life, while women like Edith Stein and M. Madeleva Wolff forged paths as writers and intellectuals who made an indelible mark on Catholicism and Christianity.

Throughout these pages, we will learn of their stories and wisdom.

The women you'll read about in these pages demonstrated a wide range of charisms. What unifies them, though, is simple: They loved God and spread the Gospel by loving others. That's a model that we can all adopt, regardless of our current life state.

Many, many women could have been featured in these pages because of their strong faith and deep love for Christ and His Church. This is just a sampling of some of the strong, faithful women of the 20th century; what the women who have been profiled here share is a relentless pursuit of God's will and a willingness to answer His call with their whole hearts.

Whether you choose to read this book straight through or a chapter at a time, I hope that you, too, will be inspired by their heroic boldness. I hope that you will take time to think about God's calling in your own life. You'll see that doing ordinary things with the intention of serving God can transform your life into something extraordinarily beautiful.

So, without further ado, let's dive in!

The Roman Catholic Church in the 20th Century

The 20th century was a time of significant movement, reform, and challenges in the Catholic Church as it sought to meet people's changing needs and realities. The 1900s saw increasing industrialization, the rise and fall of multiple communist regimes, evolving societal norms about the roles of men and women, and the deadliest wars in history, all of which impacted millions of believers. While it is impossible to adequately summarize an entire century in the life of the church in a few short paragraphs, here are some key elements that helped shape the church's response to this period.

Papal Leadership

The pontificate of Leo XIII (1878-1903) ushered in the 20th century. He is most well-known for his encyclical *Rerum Novarum* (1891), which affirmed the right to private property and called for the establishment of a living wage for workers. Next, Pius X (1903-1914) adopted a very anti-modernism stance and also enacted several liturgical reforms. He was known for his love of the poor and sick and was canonized in 1954. World War I overshadowed Benedict XV's (1914-1922) papacy as his repeated calls for peace went unheeded. He was able, however, to put an end to the anti-modernism campaign begun by Pius X.

Pius XI (1922-1939) had a great fear of Communism, which may have led him to underestimate the goals and future impact of both fascism and Naziism. His 1928 encyclical *Mortalium Animos* prohibited Catholic participation in ecumenical conferences. Pius XII (1939-1958) was pope during the turbulent years of World War

II and is often criticized for not doing enough to help the Jewish people. John XXIII (1958-1963) was one of the most beloved popes in recent history and called the Second Vatican Council (also known as Vatican II) with the goal of "bringing fresh air" into the church. He was canonized in 2014. Paul VI (1963-1978) inherited the task of completing and implementing the reforms of Vatican II. He is also widely remembered for his 1968 encyclical *Humanae Vitae*, which affirmed that sexual relations should be both unitive and procreative and thus condemned the use of artificial means of birth control. He was canonized in 2018.

John Paul I (1978) was pontiff for only 33 days before he died of a heart attack. The first Polish pope succeeded him, John Paul II (1978-2005), whose long pontificate was marked by travels and energy. He visited 129 countries, established World Youth Day, and is also credited with helping to bring an end to Soviet Communism. He was canonized in 2014.

Second Vatican Council

The Second Vatican Council, also known as Vatican II, was a hugely significant event in the life of the modern Church. Vatican II had a missionary goal, unlike earlier Church councils, which were more theological. Convened by Pope St. John XXIII in 1962, the council addressed the needs of an increasingly secular world. The council met four times in three years and concluded in 1965 during Pope St. Paul VI's papacy. Sixteen documents were drafted as a result of the council's work, including *Lumen Gentium*, which established the laity's central role in the Church's mission, and *Gaudium et Spes*, which confirmed that the Church serves the whole human family.

Vatican II also brought about liturgical reforms, including celebrating the Mass in the local language rather than Latin and a renewed emphasis on the Scriptures. The council also reaffirmed the universal call to holiness for *all* people, not only clergy or religious, and placed increased focus on lay people's participation in liturgy and ministry. In addition, Vatican II stressed the importance of ecumenism, uniting different Christian churches in both the resulting documents and also in those who participated in the council. Non-Catholics, including Protestants, Orthodox, and others, were invited to attend for the first time.

It may be said that the Church is still implementing Vatican II's work, certainly still reaping the benefits and addressing challenges from this landmark event.

Catholic Social Teaching

Catholic Social Teaching was codified in the 20th century and advocates for human rights and social justice. Pope Leo XIII's 1891 encyclical *Rerum Novarum* and Pope Pius XI's 1931 *Quadragesimo Anno* laid its foundation, which was further developed in subsequent documents.

The teaching is based on seven key themes. First, the life and dignity of the human person remind us that all human life is sacred. Second, the call to family, community, and participation tells us that humanity is not only sacred but also social. Third, rights and responsibilities confirm that we all have a right to life, accompanied by certain responsibilities. Fourth, the option for the poor and vulnerable emphasizes that "a basic moral test is how our most vulnerable members are faring," as the United States Conference of Catholic Bishops states. Fifth, the dignity of work and workers' rights confirm that work is a way to participate in God's creation and, as such, workers have certain rights and responsibilities. Sixth, solidarity reminds us that we are all brothers and sisters in our great human family, and we are indeed each other's keepers. Finally, care for God's creation points to our obligation to act as stewards of creation.

Interfaith Dialogue and Ecumenism

The 20th century saw the Catholic church reverse its position on interfaith dialogue, which it had previously not participated in or encouraged. In fact, the opening lines of the Vatican II document *Unitatis Redintegratio*, the Decree on Ecumenism, are, "The restoration of unity among all Christians is one of the principal concerns of the Second Vatican Council."

"May they all be one . . . that the world may believe that you have sent me" (John 17:21). Inspired by the gospel, with Vatican II, the church stepped off the sidelines of interfaith dialogue and into the conversation. Many believe ecumenism between Catholics and other Christian denominations, as well as Judaism, Islam, and other faiths, is one of the most visible fruits of the Council.

Challenges and Scandals

In some ways, the 20th century began with an anti-modernist, defensive posture from the Church, which sparked fierce theological debates on themes at the very heart of Catholicism. While the Second Vatican Council seemed to resolve some issues, tension about how and to what extent to implement those reforms continued throughout the rest of the century. Two major camps emerged post Vatican II - those in favor of shoring up

Church tradition and those who were interested in contemporary culture.

During the latter half of the 20th century, many complaints of clerical abuse emerged, which gained significant attention at the beginning of the 21st century. The Church enacted several processes to address these issues but continues to deal with the ramifications of these scandals even today.

Against this backdrop, and as individual threads in the fabric of the 20th-century church, the women in the following pages sought to do the right thing in their different circumstances. As the Church responded to the changes of an increasingly secular world, these women also responded to their own situations, in their own time, place, and context, to be faithful witnesses to the world they lived in.

Chapter 1:
Dorothy Day 1897-1980

United States

In History

- The Great Depression began with the U.S. stock market crash on Black Thursday, October 24, 1929, and wreaked havoc on the global economy until 1939.

- The Social Security Act was approved on August 14, 1935. For the first time, a new payroll tax was established to provide an unemployment insurance system throughout the United States and financial support for older people.

- While some American banks allowed women to have their own bank account in the 1960s, only with the passage of the Equal Credit Opportunity Act in 1974 was it regulated that women could have their own bank account and apply for credit or a mortgage.

In Society

- More and more women joined the workforce in the U.S. post-World War I, and the consumer economy and mass-produced automobiles gave people a mobility that was previously unimaginable.

- Margaret Sanger opened the first birth control clinic in the United States in Brooklyn, New York, on October 16, 1916. Women began to have access to birth control from that point forward.

- No new societal phenomena, there have been anti-war protests around every war in the United States. However, none were more organized or large-scale, as were the protests against the Vietnam War, with widespread demonstrations in the late 1960s and early 1970s.

The greatest challenge of the day is: how to bring about a revolution of the heart, a revolution which has to start with each one of us?

–Dorothy Day

Dorothy Day was the unlikely person to become one of the most famous, if not *the* most famous, American Catholic woman of the 20th century. Her practice of radical hospitality, commitment to social justice and working with the poor and marginalized continue to inspire people today. If you were to meet middle-aged Dorothy in a *Catholic Worker* house, you'd be shocked to learn of her rowdy life as a young adult, but a brief view into Dorothy's life shows the power of conversion and God's ability to transform *anyone* into a powerful advocate for the Gospel.

Early Life

Dorothy was born in 1897 in New York and moved to Oakland, California, with her family at a young age, where she lived through the great 1906 earthquake. She watched her mother and neighbors help those who became homeless due to the devastation of the earthquake, which impacted her greatly and later influenced her passion for helping those in need.

The family eventually ended up in Chicago, where Dorothy enrolled at the University of Illinois. She studied there for two years. Although she was a member of the Episcopal church as a child, she turned to socialism during her time in college and rejected organized religion altogether. When her family moved back to New York City, Dorothy dropped out of college and moved as well.

She found a job writing for a socialist newspaper, lived on the Lower East Side of Manhattan, and regularly saw deep poverty in nearby tenements—something that would later further inform her commitment to serving those in need. She also embraced a bohemian lifestyle replete with legendary bouts of drinking and relationships with various men, eventually becoming pregnant and having an illegal abortion in 1920. After some time, Dorothy met Forster Batterham, a biologist, and they settled into a common-law marriage.

Dorothy wrote and published an autobiographical novel, *The Eleventh Virgin*, in 1924. Sales of the novel, as well as the sale of the screen rights, enabled Dorothy to purchase a cottage on Staten Island, where she lived with Batterham.

The Call to Catholicism

Around this time, Dorothy started to dabble in religious practices: carrying a rosary in her pocket, displaying a statue of Mary that someone had given her, and attending Mass. Her attraction to Catholicism caused tension with Batterham, which escalated when Dorothy eventually became pregnant. In 1926, they had a daughter, Tamar, and Dorothy desired to baptize her baby in the Catholic Church.

She met a nun, Sister Aloysia, and asked about baptizing Tamar. Sister Aloysia provided basic catechetical instruction to Dorothy as a condition of her daughter's baptism, and Tamar was baptized soon after. Batterham was in and out of their lives, but eventually, Dorothy and Tamar left due to their differences in beliefs.

Dorothy Day "officially" became Catholic in 1927. She and Tamar spent some time in Mexico before returning to New York City around the start of the Great Depression. Dorothy supported herself and Tamar by writing for several publications, most notably for the Catholic magazine *Commonweal.* She covered a hunger march in Washington, D.C., in 1932 that also afforded her the opportunity to visit the Shrine of the Immaculate Conception, where she asked God to show her what He had planned for her life and her gifts as a writer and activist.

Shortly after covering the march, she met a Frenchman named Peter Maurin, who became exceptionally influential in her life. Maurin was also Catholic and taught Dorothy about the history of the Catholic Church, its social doctrines, and its saints. He voluntarily lived in poverty and had a great zeal for performing works of mercy, which impressed Dorothy. She regarded Maurin's ideas as the answer to the prayer she'd offered in Washington at the Shrine of the Immaculate Conception.

Maurin's vision of taking responsibility for those in need inspired Dorothy, and the two decided to start a newspaper, marrying Dorothy's journalistic skills with Maurin's vision of spreading Catholic social doctrine. This was the answer that Dorothy had been seeking to the question of how to use her training and her concern for social welfare to effect meaningful change.

The Rise of The Catholic Worker

Dorothy and Maurin co-founded *The Catholic Worker,* a monthly paper that tried to inspire people to volunteer to serve those in need and to promote Catholic social teaching. The first issue, published in May 1933, sold for a penny; they printed 2,500 copies. The paper soon became extremely popular, with a peak circulation of 150,000.

The Catholic Worker initially focused on the homeless and unemployed who had been affected by the Great Depression, but later, it also began to call attention to racial equality, labor disputes, and the challenges faced by migrant workers. Dorothy and Maurin believed that while works of mercy were excellent and necessary, it was equally critical to challenge the social structures that left so many people struggling and dependent upon works of mercy for food and housing. They called for a "revolution of the heart" and urged people to live out the Gospel deeply to effect societal change.

So many people were inspired by *The Catholic Worker* that volunteers and donations poured in to assist people struggling from the effects of the Depression. This led Dorothy to start Catholic Worker hospitality houses, which provided shelter and fed the poor, infirm, and unemployed. They were staffed by volunteers who lived in the houses, in poverty, alongside those they served. The first Catholic Worker House opened in New York City in 1934, and by 1939, there were 40 Catholic Worker houses in locations around the United States. Catholic Worker houses still serve those in need today; there are over 180 houses in the United States and worldwide.

Dorothy's personal and professional challenges did not end after her conversion to Catholicism. She wrote in support of racial equality, unions, and migrant workers in *The Catholic Worker*, which was not always popularly received. She was jailed several times for participating in public, nonviolent demonstrations.

She was also a committed pacifist and remained staunchly so during World War II and the Cold War. Dorothy was criticized for her ideals of nonviolence, particularly during World War II. By the end of the war, there were only 11 Catholic Worker houses still in operation, and *The Catholic Worker's* circulation had dwindled to 50,000. Nevertheless, Dorothy persisted.

Dorothy was known for the interest she showed in other people. When two former Catholic Workers spoke about this, one remarked, "One of the images I'll always have of Dorothy is of her sitting with her knitting and listening to somebody pouring out some terrible story." The other replied, "I can remember her sitting doing the same thing on Mott Street, except then she always had a cigarette in her mouth." (Hennessy, pg 97)

Personal Challenges
Dorothy also faced personal difficulties and professional criticism of her ideals. In 1943, she spent several months away from her work with *The Catholic Worker* and the Catholic Worker houses so that she could go on retreat near the boarding school that Tamar attended. Growing up in the Catholic Worker houses and sharing her mother with so many causes took a toll on their relationship. Dorothy saw her time on retreat as an

avenue for them to rekindle a strong relationship and grow close again—without the distractions and demands placed on her time by her work.

Peter Maurin died in 1949, and Dorothy felt his loss keenly. She wrote another autobiography, *The Long Loneliness*, in 1952. Despite her personal loss and the professional criticisms that she faced, Dorothy continued to write and publish *The Catholic Worker*.

Dorothy also traveled the United States to give talks that tirelessly promoted living in community, performing works of mercy, and working for peace through nonviolent means. She protested nuclear war and was arrested a couple of times during demonstrations for peace. She was part of a delegation that attended the final session of the Second Vatican Council to encourage the council to take a strong stance against nuclear weapons and in support of peace and nonviolence.

Dorothy's health began to decline in the 1970s, although she continued to travel, write, and speak as her energy permitted. She passed away in 1980, surrounded by Tamar and her family.

Her Legacy

Dorothy's cause for canonization is ongoing. She was declared a Servant of God in 2000, and the Archdiocese of New York City established the Dorothy Day Guild in 2005 to promote her canonization.

Dorothy balanced her responsibilities as a mother, a writer, a speaker, and the leader of a large charitable organization. She persevered in her strong commitment to living out her Catholic faith. Her life was radically devoted to recognizing the dignity of all people regardless of race, economic status, occupation, or home country.

Dorothy looked at the world through the lens of social justice rather than a specific political party. Her views couldn't fit into a single political "box," but rather, they focused on the inherent dignity of each person and the need to serve those most in need. She served God, not political leaders, and she wasn't afraid to voice her beliefs regardless of the political pushback.

Dorothy Day's life shows an unapologetic commitment to her beliefs, regardless of the criticism leveled by others. She spoke out boldly and frequently on topics that she believed strongly. When people censored Dorothy for her pacifism and *The Catholic Worker's* circulation declined, she refused to waver from her commitment to peace and nonviolence. When people criticized Dorothy for calling for racial equality, she stuck to her convictions that all people were created by God with equal dignity regardless of skin tone.

Dorothy's legacy lives on in her love of Scripture as well. Perhaps because she grew up as a Protestant, Dorothy had a familiarity with and hunger for Scripture that was unusual among many lay Catholics of the time. She frequently turned to Scripture for comfort and insight, such as Jesus's example of how to live in charity.

Her solidarity with the poor and working class is another source of inspiration for many. Dorothy is an example of how to engage with others to perform works of mercy personally; she practiced what she preached by living out the principles she espoused in The Catholic Worker. In addition to embracing poverty and service, Dorothy was willing to suffer for the sake of justice—whether through time in jail, physical hardship, or criticism.

Pope Francis even referenced Dorothy's legacy when addressing Congress during his visit to the United States in 2015, saying, "Her social activism, her passion for justice and for the cause of the oppressed, were inspired by the Gospel, her faith, and the example of the saints" (as cited in McNamara, 2021). Her example continues to be modern and relevant even as society changes and evolves over time.

A final but crucial piece of Dorothy's legacy is the fact that she tirelessly promoted Catholic social teaching as a lay leader. She provides an example of a committed Catholic woman who served the Church without taking religious vows or entering an order. Rather, she worked as a layperson who had tremendous influence in furthering the spread of the Gospel through serving others.

While she worked diligently to serve others and spread social justice, Dorothy also intentionally carved out time to step away from her work when she realized that her relationship with her daughter was suffering. She determined what she needed to do to balance her calling as a mother with her calling as a lay activist. She could have easily put her professional work above the needs of her daughter by citing the number of people who needed her help. Still, she realized one crucial truth: any number of people could step in to help people at the Catholic Worker houses, but only one person could be Tamar's mother.

Dorothy Day may not have considered herself extraordinary; in fact, during her lifetime, she scoffed at the idea that she would one day be known as a saint. She did what she felt needed to be done—like serving the poor, promoting justice, and working for peace—with extraordinary faith and extraordinary passion. She never let popularity or fame stand in the way of her commitment to social justice and living out Catholic social teachings.

Dorothy knew that challenging the social structures that trapped people in poverty was as important as serving them. Dorothy is an example of radical discipleship, combining faith with social action and inspiring others through the example we live out.

Servant of God Dorothy Day, pray for us!

Reflection Questions

- Dorothy Day was famous for welcoming those no one else would take in: the ungrateful, the insane, the addicted, and those with chronic problems. How do you react when you must deal with an ungrateful person?

- Dorothy struggled to balance her duties as a mother with her mission to serve the poor. Do you ever feel pulled in different directions by important areas in your life? How do you handle that?

- Dorothy's conversion from her life as a young woman to the religious social activist she became was remarkable. How have you changed as you've grown? What has surprised you most?

Chapter 2:

Margit Slachta 1884-1974

Hungary, United States

In History

- World War I raged across Europe from 1914-1918. It started following the assassination of the heir to the throne of the Austro-Hungarian Empire and quickly spread across Europe and beyond due to a web of military treaties. The Central Powers, including Germany, Austria-Hungary, Bulgaria, and the Ottoman Empire, fought the Allied Powers, including Great Britain, France, Russia, Italy, Romania, Canada, Japan, and the United States. It was the deadliest Western war in history at the time and one of the most destructive, killing more than 16 million people.

- World War II was fought from 1939-1945 and became history's biggest and deadliest war, with more than 50 countries involved. It began with the 1939 Nazi invasion of Poland and continued until the Allies defeated Nazi Germany and Japan in 1945.

- During World War II, Nazi Germany deliberately persecuted and murdered approximately six million Jews and at least five million prisoners of war, including the handicapped, homosexuals, Nazi resistors, and other victims during the Holocaust.

In Society

- After World War II, the Soviet Union established the Iron Curtain, a political barrier to seal itself and its Eastern European allies off from western and non-communist countries. It was in place until 1990.

- The Eastern bloc countries behind the Iron Curtain included Bulgaria, Czechoslovakia, East Germany, Hungary, Poland, and Romania, and were a sphere of influence for the Soviet Union. During that time, these countries modeled their government, military and foreign policies after the Soviet Union, which was their primary trade partner and from whom they received large amounts of economic aid.

- Religion was considered a competitive ideology to Communism in the Soviet areas of influence, and believers of all faiths were persecuted to eradicate religious influence in society.

I stand without compromise, on the foundation of Christian values; that is, I profess that love obliges us to accept natural laws for our fellow men without exception, which God gave and cannot be taken away.

–Sr. Margit Slachta

Hungary's first woman in Parliament, Sister Margit Slachta courageously defended human dignity regardless of social standing, ethnicity, or religious beliefs. She was simultaneously a woman of God and a woman of the world, uniting political work with a deep spirituality in an environment torn apart by hatred and violence.

Early Life

Born in Hungary in 1884, it was evident that Margit would leave an indelible mark on society, namely politics. She and her parents spent a short time in the U.S. but later returned to Hungary. There, Margit pursued degrees in French and German from a school in Budapest and joined the Society of the Social Mission in 1908. She was interested in politics, particularly in working to improve the situation of women and children. To that end, she helped start the Union of Catholic Women—later known as the Party of Christian Women—and focused on calling attention to women and the challenges they faced at work and home. She wanted to help women both by alleviating the difficulties they encountered and by addressing the social systems that caused those issues in the first place.

The Political Religious

Sr. Margit's political interest deepened, and she was elected as the first female member of Hungary's Parliament in 1920. She used her seat in Parliament to continue bringing attention to women and children and their needs. Sr. Margit's political work was not driven by a quest for power, fame, and influence. Rather, she saw her political position as a way to serve God by calling others to recognize the dignity of every human being, particularly those who were overlooked. For Sr. Margit, becoming the first female member of Parliament was never the goal. Instead, she aimed to serve others and demonstrate a true Christian love of one's neighbors.

In 1923, in addition to her political activities, Sr. Margit founded the Sisters of Social Service. The order began in Budapest, and the sisters were often called the "gray nuns" because of their gray habits. Somewhat uniquely, the sisters took annual vows rather than perpetual vows, which is more common in most religious orders.

Sr. Margit saw work as a type of prayer and instilled this same ideal into the Sisters of Social Service. The Sisters had particular charisms for nursing, midwifery, and care of orphans. They performed works of charity, especially among the poor, and also were actively involved in social issues and various social action movements.

Opposition to the Spread of Naziism

As World War II began and various groups of people, especially Jews, faced oppression, Sr. Margit became more politically outspoken. Hungary passed its first set of anti-Jewish laws in 1938. Sr. Margit had started a newspaper called *The Voice of the Spirit* and began publishing articles that vehemently decried the antisemitic laws and sentiment in Hungary.

She also strongly denounced the Nazi party and Nazi beliefs, arguing that they were both spiritually and morally bankrupt. Sr. Margit observed that Nazism pushed people to abandon their church and their community. She pointed out that Nazi beliefs lacked understanding of God's love, overwrote Biblical teaching, and went so far as to deny God's existence because for the Nazis, power and control were the ultimate ideal.

The Nazi party had gained enough power and influence in Europe—particularly in Eastern Europe—that expressing views denouncing the Nazi belief system could be dangerous. The Hungarian government warned her about her opinions and tried to suppress *The Voice of the Spirit,* so Sr. Margit took its publication underground. She refused to let governmental intimidation stand in the way of her beliefs about what was right.

The Hungarian government quickly moved from passing anti-Jewish laws to arresting and deporting Jewish people. In 1940, Sr. Margit and the Sisters of Social Service encountered a group of Jews from Csíkszereda who had been transported to the Hungarian-Romanian-Russian border. They were being kept in abject poverty and deplorable conditions, faced with the choice of trying to survive the winter where they were or fleeing into the

Russian woods and trying to make a life for themselves there.

Sr. Margit wrote to several priests and asked for assistance for this group of Jewish families. Because of her efforts, they were eventually released. The Hungarian authorities, facing increased pressure from Germany, began "resettling" Jewish people in huge numbers in 1941. Over 20,000 Jews were deported in just a two-month period. Sr. Margit vehemently protested this as well. She wrote to Hungarian officials and called the "resettlement" a contradiction of the commandments of God.

After the "resettlement," SS units eventually murdered almost 14,000 Hungarian Jews in a mass killing. Sr. Margit, along with several others, tried to visit the mass grave, but they were denied permission to go near the site. After seeing the Nazis murder so many Jewish people, the Hungarian government turned to using them as slave laborers rather than handing them over to the Nazis. Sr. Margit continued to protest the government's treatment of the Jews in Hungary. She wrote letters, gave speeches, and published articles denouncing what was happening.

In 1942, Sr. Margit got word of further deportations. She and the other Sisters of Social Service raised the issue to a local priest and archdeacon, urging them to act with merciful compassion to try to protect the Jewish people. In 1943, Sr. Margit appealed directly to Pope Pius XII to try to stop the deportations from occurring. This appeal has been largely credited for delaying many deportations.

Sr. Margit was warned about her pro-Jewish stance many times, but she continued publishing *The Voice of the Spirit* underground. She also used a film and lecture series to try to counter Nazi propaganda and educate the Hungarian people about what was happening in hopes that they would speak out to protect the Jews and other people targeted by the Nazi party.

The Nazis took over Budapest in 1944. Jewish people were forced into ghettos, and Sr. Margit and her Sisters turned their attention to serving in those ghettos. They gave up their gray habits and started wearing secular clothing so that they could pass in and out of the ghettos without drawing attention to themselves. The Sisters hid an estimated 1,000 Jews during the Nazi occupation in Budapest and served food to an estimated 2,000 people daily. They brought medicine, food, and clothing to the people there.

Even though many Hungarian Christians stopped publicly supporting the Jewish people once the Nazis took over Budapest because it was too dangerous, the Sisters of Social Service increased their efforts to serve the Jews. They viewed the Jewish families in the ghettos as God among them.

It's estimated that the Sisters of Social Service saved over 2,000 Hungarian Jews from death during World War II. They hid Jewish people, worked with the Holy Cross Society to baptize Jewish families who had converted to Christianity, and provided food, supplies, and medicine—all without heed to the danger that this placed them in. One of the Sisters, Sr. Sára Salkaházi, was murdered after their house in Budapest was searched, and Sr. Margit herself was badly beaten at one point.

Nevertheless, Sr. Margit and her Sisters trusted in God and carried out their work with deep, abiding faith.

A Brief Return to Politics

After World War II ended, Sr. Margit returned to Parliament. She particularly focused on defending the Church and promoting religious freedom. She opposed Communist views and the dictatorships springing up in Eastern Europe. Sr. Margit forcefully protested Hungary's decision to nationalize church schools, going so far as to stay seated during the national anthem. She was eventually banned from Parliament for six months due to her protests.

As the political climate in Hungary continued to evolve and Communism took hold more and more deeply, Sr. Margit eventually emigrated to the United States for her safety. She and her sister came to the U.S. in 1949, settling in Buffalo, New York, where a group of the Sisters of Social Service had been established in the 1920s. The Sisters' governance moved to Buffalo along with her; although the order was still active in Hungary, it was forced underground in the 1950s due to Communist rule. Sr. Margit died in Buffalo in 1974 and was buried there. In 2021, she was exhumed and reburied in Budapest.

Her Legacy

Sr. Margit was awarded the title "Righteous Among the Nations" by Yad Vashem, the World Holocaust Remembrance Center, in 1985. This title is given to people who are recognized as having risked their lives to save Jews during the Holocaust. Her life is the subject of the documentary project *Angel of Mercy* by filmmaker George Csicsery.

The Sisters of the Social Service still exist today, and the order is active in nine countries on three continents. True to Sr. Margit's original vision, the order works to spread God's love and promote social justice.

Sr. Margit Slachta is an inspirational figure in many ways. As the first female member of the Hungarian Parliament, she boldly challenged the social norms of the time and proved that women can work alongside men in matters of governance. As the founder of a religious order, she's also inspiring for her willingness to answer God's call to protect human dignity despite political and life-threatening challenges.

By combining both of these identities, Sr. Margit gives us a beautiful example of someone who was politically savvy, involved in the culture around her, and also highly attuned to spiritual life. She shattered the stereotype of the "hidden nun" whose external activities are limited. Instead, Sr. Margit participated in organized politics at a high level and was active in social causes. She worked to improve the situation of women and children before calling attention to the inhumane treatment of the Jewish people during World War II.

She saw human rights as a spiritual issue, not only a political issue, and allowed her Catholic faith to guide her in fighting for those whose rights were being unjustly taken away. While Sr. Margit was part of the governing body in Hungary, she felt that God's laws unquestionably transcended man's laws. Therefore, if the government made laws that were in contradiction to God's law, those laws were unjust and should be opposed.

Sr. Margit shows us that a "both/and" spirituality is possible: We can be active in the world and also active in the life of the spirit. As a politician and religious sister, she bridged the gap that often divides worldly and spiritual leadership. She saw her political activities as an avenue of spiritual ministry. Sr. Margit believed that she served by using her God-given talents in her political role to uplift the lives and voices of the unheard.

Impressively, Sr. Margit served in this role regardless of the political and physical risk. She refused to let her voice be suppressed even when her opinions were unpopular or put her in danger. Instead, she trusted God and boldly continued to proclaim human dignity and the need to treat others with love and compassion.

Sr. Margit's courage and conviction are a potent testament to what can happen when ordinary people put their desire for God above their thirst for power, status, and influence. Sr. Margit let her desire for God guide the way she used her political power and influence; instead of staying content with the status quo, she strove to make Hungary a better place for everyone—not just the wealthy and the politically connected.

Sr. Margit also shows us what is possible when we put our faith in God despite the risks that we face, either personally, professionally, or politically. She never wavered in her commitment to living out Christian love and service, and her unwavering faith allowed her to perform heroic acts. She saw these heroic actions as simply "doing the right thing," and her example can inspire us to courageously do the right thing in whatever situation we may be facing.

Sr. Margit Slachta, pray for us!

Reflection Questions

- Sr. Margit was very politically savvy and very spiritually mature. Do your religious beliefs inform your political beliefs? How so?

- Sr. Margit was curious to know if she would ever see Hungary again when she left in 1949. Have you had to give up something or someone dear to you to continue your God-given mission? If so, how did you handle this? If not, how do you think you would react?

- Sr. Margit married acts of service with evangelizing words in her speeches and in *The Voice of the Spirit.* Do you serve with both acts of service and also with evangelizing words? Is one easier for you than the other?

Chapter 3:
Mother Teresa of Calcutta 1910-1997
Macedonia, India
In History

- On August 15, 1947, India and Pakistan gained independence from the British Empire after 200 years of British rule. This was due to several factors, including the British no longer being able to sustain the empire financially following World War II.

- The British transferred power to the newly established Indian government in less than six months in light of the growing independence movement and increasing violence. This led to handoffs that were largely not well planned and often haphazard.

- India was partitioned into two countries, the Republic of India and the Islamic Republic of Pakistan, and religious violence broke out as communities sought to establish themselves. The Hindu faithful were the majority in India, while Muslim believers were the majority in Pakistan.

In Society

- The effects of both World War II and the partition of India and Pakistan led to mass migration and a refugee crisis in those areas, as more than 14 million people left their homes to find refuge.

- Mohandas Karamchand Gandhi, known as Mahatma, led India's nonviolent campaign of passive resistance against colonial British rule. He was known for his Hindu faith and ascetic lifestyle and was arrested several times for his efforts towards Indian independence. He was assassinated in 1948 by a Hindu fanatic as he worked toward peace between Hindus and Muslims.

- In the 20th century, the global population quadrupled, with Asia seeing explosive growth and the greatest change in its demographics of any other continent.

Not all of us can do great things. But we can do small things with great love.

–Mother Teresa

Ask anyone—whether Catholic, Christian, or nonreligious—about the most influential religious leaders of the 20th century, and there's a good chance that Mother Teresa of Calcutta will be at or near the top of their list. She's not just one of the most recognizable saints of the 20th century; she's one of the most recognizable people of the 20th century, period. Her smiling face and blue-and-white sari are even identifiable among those with no religious affiliation, and her influence still resonates globally.

Early Life

Mother Teresa was born Agnes Gonxha Bojaxhiu in 1910 in Uskup, Ottoman Empire, now Skopje, North Macedonia, to Macedonian parents. Her father died when she was just eight years old, and young Agnes was very close with her mother and watched as she invited others, especially the poor, into their home for meals. Her family strongly advocated for charity and hospitality to those most in need.

She first felt the call to religious life when she was only 12 years old and entered the Sisters of Loreto in 1928 when she was 18. She spent her initial years in the order in Ireland, and then, after professing her first vows in 1931 and taking the name Sister Mary Teresa, she was sent to Calcutta, India. She taught at a high school, St. Mary's, that served girls from Calcutta's poor families and there she learned to speak both Bengali and Hindi. She took final vows in 1937; it was at this time that she received the title "Mother"—which was the customary title for the Sisters of Loreto after their final vows—and became known by the name "Mother Teresa."

The Call Within a Call

Several years after professing her final vows, in 1944, Mother Teresa became the principal of St. Mary's High School. Just a few years later, her life was changed when she received what she referred to as her "call within a call." Mother Teresa was traveling by train to make a retreat when she heard Christ call her to leave the school, go out to the slums, and assist the poorest of the poor.

However, because her religious vows included a vow of obedience, she did not leave her convent immediately. It took two more years before Mother Teresa received official permission to leave her convent. So, in 1948, Mother Teresa received six months of basic medical training, donned the blue and white sari that would eventually become internationally known, and headed out to the slums of Calcutta.

The Missionaries of Charity

Mother Teresa started her ministry with an informal, open-air school. Soon, through the grace of God, she convinced the government to give her a run-down building that she turned into a home for the dying. She picked people up out of the gutters and brought them back to this home so that they could die with dignity, knowing that someone saw them and loved them.

Other women soon followed Mother Teresa, and the Missionaries of Charity received canonical recognition in 1950. The order grew quickly, both in terms of vocations and donations, and soon was able to expand and serve more and more people. The order also opened its first home outside Calcutta in 1950.

Throughout the 1950s and 1960s, more and more houses were opened in Calcutta and other parts of India. They served the poor, the dying, the blind, the elderly, the disabled, lepers, and orphans—in essence, anyone who was viewed as unwanted or a burden by the society around them.

The Missionaries of Charity Brothers was founded by Mother Teresa in 1963, and contemplative branches of the order followed in later years. The Brothers and the contemplative branches helped to address different types of poverty as the order's mission expanded. In 1965, the Missionaries of Charity received a Decree of Praise from Pope Paul VI, allowing them to expand internationally. Mother Teresa began attracting global attention for her work with the poor and her desire to minister to the most forgotten and abandoned. In fact, she received the Nobel Peace Prize for her work in 1979.

Also, in 1979, the Missionaries of Charity opened a house in Croatia and were able to begin ministering in Communist countries; the order eventually had houses in almost every Communist country other than China. Houses in the United States were opened specifically to serve AIDS patients starting in 1985. Mother Teresa's charism of service, joy, and doing small things with great love always imbued the houses and the members of the Missionaries.

Mother Teresa spent the 1980s and 1990s traveling the world to serve the poor. She opened new Missionaries of Charity houses and spoke to the public about faith, morals, and service. She was never afraid to venture into any area of the world, no matter how dangerous. She even visited active war zones, such as Beirut in 1982, when she traveled to rescue children from the fighting there. Mother Teresa always trusted God to make a way for her and to keep her safe.

Speaking Out

During her travels and her speeches, Mother Teresa exhorted people to serve the poor. She also frequently pointed out that the greatest poverty was spiritual poverty and that feeling unloved was worse than material poverty. Mother Teresa was as concerned with feeding people's souls as she was with feeding their bodies; her ministry was both spiritual and corporeal.

In addition to the Nobel Peace Prize, Mother Teresa received many other humanitarian awards, including the Bharat Ratna—the highest honor given to civilians in India—the Pope John XXIII Peace Prize, and the Nehru Prize.

However, Mother Teresa's outspokenness on certain topics caused some to view her as a controversial figure. She unabashedly spoke out against abortion, contraception, and divorce, in addition to her work promoting peace and charity. Despite criticism, she continued to uphold Catholic teachings about these topics until the end of her life. She boldly declared God's truth and His universal call to holiness, no matter what other people thought or said about her.

Mother Teresa died in 1997, leaving a legacy of over 4,000 Missionaries of Charity serving in 610 foundations in 123 countries. Hundreds of thousands of people in India attended her funeral procession and state funeral.

How does someone become a canonized saint?

There are several steps to becoming an official, canonized saint in the church. The first step occurs at least five years after someone's death, and in this phase the local diocese examines the person's life. If they are found to have lived a virtuous life, their cause is sent to the Vatican's Congregation for the Causes of Saints and the person is called a **Servant of God.**

The next step in the road to sainthood includes three layers of approvals. Theologians look at the evidence gathered in the first phase of the process and if they agree with the diocesan findings, they share their recommendation with the Congregation. If the members of the Congregation also agree, the case is sent to the Pope for his approval. If the Pope also approves, the person is now called **Venerable** *if they lived a virtuous life, or* **Blessed** *if they were martyred.*

In the next stage, a miracle must be attributed to the person's intercession. If a miracle is approved, the person is now called **Blessed.** *Finally, to move onto canonization, a second miracle must be confirmed. If/when this occurs, the person is called a* **Saint.**

The Saint of the Gutters

Mother Teresa was named a Servant of God in 1999. Typically, there is a five-year waiting period after a person's death before they are eligible to be declared a Servant of God, but Pope John Paul II gave a special dispensation to the "Saint of the Gutters" and declared her a Servant of God just two years after her death.

She was beatified in 2003 after a woman in India was miraculously cured of cancer through Mother Teresa's intercession, becoming the quickest person to receive beatification in the history of the Catholic Church. Mother Teresa was officially named a saint in 2016 after a man in Brazil—who had been in a coma—was healed of brain tumors after his family prayed for Mother Teresa's aid.

Like St. Thérèse of Lisieux—whose name she chose upon making her religious vows—Mother Teresa did small things that she transformed into great things by infusing them with great love. Teaching a girl in poverty to read or caring for a dying person may not seem extraordinary. However, by performing such actions with humility and love, knowing that to serve the person in front of you is to serve the Lord, Mother Teresa showed the world that no action is too small or insignificant to become holy. She inspired huge numbers of people to take small actions in service of others.

She earned global acclaim not for one grandiose accomplishment, but for doing simple things as though they were grandiose. Mother Teresa's ministry reminds us that each person is valuable and dignified, not because of what they have or what they've accomplished, but because they are a child of God. She loved boldly and proclaimed God's love boldly through her actions, letting them speak more profoundly than words ever could. It's no wonder that many people called her a living saint in the latter years of her life.

Heroic Perseverance

On their own, Mother Teresa's actions are inspiring enough as an example of loving like Christ. But what makes them even more exceptional is the fact that Mother Teresa radiated the love of Christ despite suffering an inner spiritual dryness that lasted almost 50 years.

Letters published after her death revealed that shortly after her ministry on the streets of Calcutta began, Mother Teresa stopped feeling the presence of God. She felt abandoned and struggled through a spiritual desert for years on end, experiencing consolation only for a few short weeks in 1959.

Mother Teresa's spiritual dryness led to feelings of doubt in her faith and even in the existence of God. To say that she underwent a profound dark night of the soul might understate just how much spiritual difficulty she experienced. Yet, Mother Teresa persevered heroically. She never stopped seeking God and seeking to do His work despite the great spiritual darkness that she faced.

In fact, Mother Teresa compared her own spiritual desolation to the loneliness and sense of being unloved that many of the people she ministered to faced. While her sense of abandonment pained her greatly, she understood it to be her way of sharing in Christ's suffering during the Passion. She used her experience to deepen her empathy for the people she served. This is true saintliness in action!

Her Legacy

Many of us have experienced periods of spiritual dryness. Her life reminds us that we don't have to "feel" God's presence to go about His work. Sometimes, grace abounds deeply even when we don't feel its presence at all.

Above all, Mother Teresa shows us, in ways too numerous to count, how one person's small, local actions can ripple outward and impact the entire world. The individual things she did—teaching children, feeding the hungry, praying with the dying—may have been ordinary, but their cumulative impact is undoubtedly extraordinary. There is nothing too insignificant for God, and Mother Teresa's life is a shining witness to what can happen when we are willing to surrender radically our lives and our daily actions to Him.

Saint Mother Teresa of Calcutta, pray for us!

Reflection Questions

- Mother Teresa suffered a decades-long dark night of the soul, when she did not feel God's presence or consolation. Have you experienced periods of spiritual dryness? If so, describe your experience. Know that you are not alone.

- Mother Teresa received not one but two vocational calls. Do you feel God calling you on a certain path? Challenging a particular belief?

- Mother Teresa was sometimes criticized for her outspokenness. What do you do when you need to share an uncomfortable truth or unpopular opinion?

Chapter 4:
Sofía del Valle 1891-1982

Mexico

In History

- The United Nations was founded in 1945, shortly before the end of World War II. Ravaged by war, representatives from 50 countries met in San Francisco to establish an international organization that, they hoped, would prevent another world war like what they had just lived through.

- Established soon after the United Nations in 1945, UNESCO is the United Nations Educational, Scientific and Cultural Organization. Its mission is to foster peace through mutual understanding and dialogue between peoples and cultures.

- UNESCO has been active in Mexico since 1967, supporting projects in education, science, culture communication, and information.

In Society

- Travelers in the early 20th century had one option for a trans-Atlantic journey - a ship. Those who were traveling cross-country had options including a horse-drawn carriage, car, or train.

- Brothers Orville and Wilbur Wright flew the first airplane on December 17, 1903. The world's first airline, the regional German company DELAG, was founded not long after in 1909. However, it was not until mid-century that airlines had their boom, and travel by airplane was widely available.

- The RMS Titanic, the largest ocean liner of its time, sank on April 14-15, 1912, after hitting an iceberg while crossing the Atlantic Ocean. Approximately 1,500 of its 2,240 passengers died in the accident.

For me, one of the most valuable and least practiced virtues is gratitude.

–Sofía del Valle

When we think about vocation, most of us typically default to considering either a vocation to marriage or a vocation to religious life. But some women, like Sofía del Valle, remind us of the tremendous impact that can be made by someone with a vocation for the single life.

Early Life

Sofía del Valle was the daughter of Europeans who had immigrated to Mexico. Her mother was born in Mexico but was of French and English descent. Her father was Spanish. The family had eight children; Sofía, born in 1891, was the second-oldest and her family nicknamed her "Chofi." Her family was wealthy; due to their financial status, as well as their fair skin and European heritage, they enjoyed quite a bit of racial and class privilege.

The del Valle family was ardently Catholic and very loving, although Sofía's strong personality often caused conflict with her mother. Her father was very tender and put a strong value on education for all of his children, boys and girls alike. Sofía was educated in European Catholic schools and eventually earned a degree in French. She spoke Spanish, French, and English and was especially devoted to St. Thérèse of Lisieux.

Thanks to their financial means, the family left Mexico City and returned to Europe in 1907, just as the Mexican Revolution was gathering strength. They spent time living in both Spain and Switzerland, where Sofía worked as a catechist and social worker.

In 1918, the family moved to Louisiana before ultimately returning to Mexico City in 1922—although some of Sofía's siblings remained in both Spain and Louisiana. However, when the family returned they'd lost much of their wealth and property as a result of the Mexican Revolution.

Societal Upheaval

While the del Valles lived abroad, the Mexican Revolution raged from 1910–1917, as long-oppressed people rebelled against dictator Porfirio Díaz. The Revolution resulted in millions of deaths and hundreds of thousands of displaced people. The Constitution of 1917 included quite a few anticlerical provisions, and more were added later, which then fanned the flames of the Cristero War in the late 1920s.

When Sofía and her family returned to Mexico in 1922, she was 30 years old. The country was in the midst of reconstruction, and there was a huge divide between the wealthy and the poor. The role of the Catholic Church in Mexican society was also changing rapidly.

Sofía found a job working for the Mexican branch of Ericsson Telephones. She also became involved with the emerging Catholic social justice movement. Between the changes wrought by the Mexican Revolution and the Industrial Revolution, it was apparent that it wasn't enough anymore for rich Catholics to give alms to the poor and assume that would fix everything. A deeper societal change was needed; Sofía recognized this but wasn't sure what to do.

Upon the recommendation of a friend, Sofía went to hear Father Mendez Medina speak. Father Medina was the director of the Mexican Social Secretariat, who advocated for a Catholic approach to labor rights and reducing class conflict. But he didn't have anyone to help organize women workers so Sofía offered to help. Little did she know that would set her life's calling in motion.

Getting Started

Sofía worked at Ericsson in the morning and for the Mexican Social Secretariat at night. She helped organize female factory workers, and she started a night school to help the workers become literate. The women paid a small fee that was pooled together and used for childcare. Through the Social Secretariat, the women could also access a food pantry and a savings and loans program. As Sofía saw the work of the Secretariat progress, she became thoroughly convinced that women needed education.

Sofía was also a member of the *Unión de Damas Católicas* and helped influence the management practices of several businesses, including factories making clothing, perfume and cigarettes.

During this time, the social upheaval in Mexico continued. When Plutarco Elías Calles became president in 1924, he introduced even more anticlerical laws designed to heavily reduce (if not completely eliminate) the Catholic Church's influence in Mexico. These laws eventually sparked the Cristero War, which started in 1926 and pitted the Mexican government against the Catholic Church.

Both sides wanted to influence what Mexico would be like after the Mexican Revolution of the 1910s. The secularist, revolutionary view wanted the Church's presence to be eradicated from Mexico, while many Catholics felt that removing the Catholic faith from Mexico would mean losing Mexico's history. They fought for religious liberty. While the Cristero War is not well known today, it made international headlines then.

The Church was forced to largely go underground. Public Masses were not held from 1926–1929, and Catholics worshiped in private. In the midst of the Cristero War, a priest named Father Miguel Miranda became head of the Mexican Social Secretariat. He soon became Sofía's spiritual director as well.

The First Liberal Arts School to Educate Women

Together, Sofía and Miranda founded the first Catholic, liberal arts institute of higher education in Mexico for women: the *Instituto Superior de Cultura Femenina* (ISCF) or the Advanced Institute of Feminine Culture. Sofía was also instrumental in starting a Catholic association for young Mexican women called *Juventud Católica Femenina Mexicana* (JCFM), which grew from just five members at its founding in 1926 to over 100,000 members by 1942. JCFM encouraged its members to combine Catholicism with work in society.

The Institute and the JCFM were allowed to continue operating during the Cristero War, even though the Church had been forced underground. Although many Catholics had taken up arms against the government to defend their religious freedom, Sofía remained a pacifist. She saw her role in the conflict as an educator of women to prepare them for the future.

Sofía gradually took on more of a leadership role within the Institute of Feminine Culture as Father Miranda started to travel extensively. Although it was unusual at the time for any woman to lead an organization without a male assisting her, Sofía rose to the challenge with grace despite her doubts that she was capable of fulfilling this large and important role.

Finally, the government and the Catholic Church negotiated a peace agreement in 1929, ending the Cristero War. But Sofía's work to educate and inform Mexican Catholic women was far from over.

Becoming the Voice of Mexican Catholics Abroad

Sofía spent some time in Europe, both for training and to regain her health, which had deteriorated under the tremendous stress and pressure of running a Catholic training institution in the midst of an anticlerical revolution. Sofía also joined the International Union of Catholic Women's Leagues.

Religious unrest continued in the 1930s, and Sofía began traveling extensively in both Europe and the U.S. with the goal of raising money and bringing awareness to the struggles that Mexican Catholics faced. She visited major capital cities like Rome, Paris, Washington, D.C., and metropolitan centers like Warsaw, Havana, and Des Moines.

Because she was a woman, she could travel extensively without falling under suspicion from the Mexican government of being involved in anything too "political." As one biographer put it, "Sofía del Valle—not a bishop, a priest, or nun, but a single woman—became the leading spokesperson for the Mexican Catholic Church in the United States and Europe" (Andes, 2019). Her femininity was a true asset to her work.

Sofía established a huge network in the U.S. and Europe through her travels. She made a trip to the U.S. almost every year for a period of about 20 years specifically to talk about the church in Mexico and the difficulties faced by Mexican Catholics. In 1939 she became the sole Latin American on the International Union of Catholic Women's Leagues leadership council, which represented 25 million women.

But her work in Mexico didn't stop once she started traveling internationally. She also traveled across Mexico, visiting cities and small towns to promote women's education. Sofía helped start a women's magazine called *Juventad*, which published articles about both Catholicism and popular culture.

Sofía's Role Evolves

During World War II, there was greater peace between the Mexican government and the Catholic Church. Sofía urged Mexican Catholics to support the government's efforts in the war. This eventually led her to a position as a liaison between the government and Catholic activist workers; Sofía helped promote economic development as part of this role. Through her travels and her activism, Sofía got to know other prominent women of the time, like Dorothy Day and Maria von Trapp.

She also spent over 25 years working as a Catholic Action delegate with UNESCO. Sofía promoted foreign relations and helped administer literary programs funded by the Mexican government in various parts of Mexico during the 1950s and 1960s. Her passion for education (and particularly women's education) as a means of closing the gap between the wealthy elite and the working class never waned.

Sofía's health began to decline in the 1970s, and as a result, she greatly reduced her activist work. Her health was very poor by 1980, and she died in Mexico in 1982 after spending a year in a nursing home in Cuernavaca.

Her Legacy

Sofía truly serves as a role model for Catholic activists, particularly female activists. She was intelligent, culturally aware, poised, and confident in her mission. Sofía showed the world that women can rise up to become leaders in both social activism and missionary work: not to replace men, but to work alongside them and add another layer of depth and understanding to the work.

The work that Sofía did to raise awareness and promote education laid a foundation for much of the activism that began to arise in the 1960s. Her activities were a model for promoting social justice through organizing the laity. Sofía promoted the Church but did so from outside the clerical hierarchy and showed the world that women can serve the Church as laypersons, not only by becoming a nun and entering consecrated religious life.

Sofía never justified her decision to remain a laywoman or devalued her work because she wasn't a wife and mother—the norm at the time. She was confident in her role and understood the tremendous impact of her work. Sofía's life is a beautiful inspiration to us to be confident with the role that God has handed us, whatever that is, and to never doubt the impact that we can have by living out our vocation. It doesn't matter if our vocation looks just like everyone else's or if it is radically different.

Sofía also practiced gratitude. Even though her work was challenging and she faced all sorts of obstacles, she was grateful for the role that the Lord gave to her and for the impact that she was able to have. She didn't just talk about living out the virtues; she practiced what she preached. That lesson applies today, just as much as it did in Sofía's own time.

Sofía's life also has tremendous parallels with today's world in another sense. She lived through huge societal changes due to advances in communication, the rise of transnationalism, and the increasing prevalence of technology. That sounds a lot like today's globally connected, technologically driven world! She navigated through understanding how Catholicism was changed by globalism and shared globally how Catholicism was important locally.

Sofía played a huge role in planting the seeds for laywomen to claim their position in the life of the Church. She showed that being a Catholic and being an activist don't have to be disparate roles; in fact, they should be deeply intertwined. Her faith grounded her professional work when she raised funds and awareness for Mexican Catholics, but that wasn't the only way that faith and activism were linked in Sofía's life.

Her faith also spurred her to advocate for women's education and workers' rights. Sofía saw that women had an important role to play in the Church, whether they were consecrated religious or part of the laity, and she also knew that educating women helped open up their horizons and improve their lives. She also recognized the dignity offered by work done well and the importance of honoring the contributions made by all types of workers. Her faith and Catholic understanding of human dignity formed the foundation for her activism in every arena.

Above all, Sofía trained women to be leaders in their homes, workplaces, societies, and even the Church. She encouraged their boldness. Through Sofía's story, we can be inspired to follow her example and encourage women to speak and lead boldly.

Sofía del Valle, pray for us!

Reflection Questions

- Sofía did not fit the typical mold of womanhood in her time and context, but she did not doubt her role. In fact, when asked why she never married or entered religious life, she simply answered that she did not feel called to either one. Are you confident in the vocation God has called you to? Why or why not?

- Sofía had to step in to lead the Institute of Feminine Culture school while Fr. Miranda traveled, whether she wanted to or not. Have you had to lead something before you felt you were ready? How did it go?

- Sofía traveled alone extensively to seek support for Mexican Catholics and was sometimes intimidated by the people she met. Despite this, she persisted in her efforts. How do you overcome your own doubts and fears to persevere in your efforts?

Chapter 5:
Edith Stein (Sr. Teresa Benedicta of the Cross) 1891-1942

Germany

In History

- In the early 20th century, Kaiser Wilhelm II ruled Germany, a relatively new nation. The unification of 25 German-speaking kingdoms and city states only occurred in the late 19th century. Wilhelm II had ambitions of growing Germany's global influence. The country had advanced technologies and industries and also had strong currents of militarism, nationalism, and government authoritarianism.

- Germany was pulled into World War I through its alliance with Austria-Hungary, which was part of its complex web of alliances to avoid a war on two fronts simultaneously with France and Russia. Obviously, this policy was not successful as more and more countries honored their treaties and declared war on the enemies of their allies.

- On the losing side of World War I, Kaiser Wilhelm was forced to abdicate. The Treaty of Versailles (1919) ordered Germany to pay steep war reparations, reduce the size of its military, and lose territory. The German economy suffered greatly, with the runaway inflation of the early

1920s devolving into a complete economic collapse at the onset of the Great Depression.

In Society

- With unemployment around 35% and shortages of basic commodities including food, Adolf Hitler took advantage of the public frustration and anger to bring the Nazi party to the political forefront by 1932.

- Antisemitism was promoted by the Nazis through organized propaganda and educational programs, in which the Jewish people were blamed for the economic, political and ethical problems in Germany. In the chaotic environment of the 1930s, their efforts were highly successful.

- The Nazis used children's programs to indoctrinate German youth with their ideology. The two primary Nazi youth organizations were the Hitler Youth for boys and the League of German Girls for girls. In 1936, membership became obligatory. The programs offered activities like sports, camping and physical exercise in addition to instruction about Nazi beliefs.

Every time I feel my powerlessness and inability to influence people directly, I become more keenly aware of the necessity of my own holocaust.

–Edith Stein

There are many reasons why Edith Stein should not have become one of the greatest Catholic thinkers of the 20th century. She was born and raised Jewish. She was a woman at a time of male dominance in intellectual circles and in academia. She became an atheist as a teenager. And yet, in her quest for truth, she also became a Carmelite nun who is recognized for her contributions to philosophy and to Catholic thought.

Growing Up Jewish

Edith was born in 1891 in Germany to orthodox Jewish parents, though her father died when she was just two. Her mother was very devout and continued to raise Edith in the Jewish faith. However, she decided she was an atheist from the time she was 13 until she turned 21— although, during this period, she was still always drawn to seek out the truth. In fact, it was this desire for truth that laid the seeds of her eventual conversion to Christianity.

Edith studied first at the University of Breslau before transferring to the University of Göttingen. She finished her degree in 1915 and then served as a nurse in a field hospital during World War I. After the war, she worked for Professor Edmund Husserl as a research assistant. She'd studied under Husserl at the University of Göttingen and was heavily influenced by his argument that objective truth can and does exist.

Husserl's case for the validity of objective truth led Edith to realize that religious experience was a valid thing to study and was part of the human experience, thus starting to crack her atheistic views. Although Husserl wasn't Catholic, his philosophical ideas started introducing her to many of the ideas contained within Christianity and Catholicism—paving the way for her later conversion.

Edith finished her doctoral work in 1917; she continued working for Husserl until 1918, when she broke off on her own. Despite her intellectual gifts and impressive academic record, she had trouble finding an academic position. Due to Germany's ruined economy in the years after World War I, such posts were difficult for men to obtain, let alone for a Jewish woman.

Edith joined the Social Democrats and began to dabble in feminist thought and topics, continued to search for truth and meaning, and in time, she became Christian. She read Teresa of Avila's autobiography in 1921, and it affected her so profoundly that she asked a priest about being baptized the very next day. She was eventually baptized on New Year's Day in 1922.

Her family, and particularly her mother, found Edith's conversion to Christianity and Catholicism hard to accept. It was very difficult for Edith to tell her mother about her conversion. Her sister Rosa also eventually converted to Catholicism. However, although she and her mother still loved each other deeply, there was a divide between Edith and the rest of the family for the rest of her life due to their divergent religious beliefs.

Edith's Life as a Catholic

After her baptism, Edith wanted to become a Carmelite nun, but her spiritual director counseled her against it and encouraged her to keep speaking, writing, and exploring philosophical ideas. Her spiritual director also helped her find a position teaching at a school for girls.

Unfortunately, this role did not fit Edith's talents. Her students found her rigid, critical, and unapproachable, and they struggled to connect with her. Edith's intellect was admirable, but her pedagogy was rather lacking. During this time, she spent hours praying and began translating the works of great Catholic thinkers and writers into German.

She began with translations of some of Cardinal Newman's writings, but they were translated so literally and so mechanically that the result was not easy to read. Next, she grappled with Thomas Aquinas' writing, particularly with one of his works that had never been translated into German before.

His theology greatly appealed to her intellect, and Edith began to lecture on Aquinas's work in 1928. She also spoke about women's place in society and women's role in the church, arguing that women should not be prohibited from active ministry and that their roles as nurses and teachers, for example, had been a vibrant part of the early Church. She outlined the difference between man-made laws and divine law, then pointed out the ways in which women's exclusion from certain spheres was due to man-made law rather than divine law.

Edith received a position at the German Institute for Educational Studies at Münster in 1932, even as Nazism and antisemitism were sharply on the rise. She realized that the Jewish people would soon, in her estimation, receive Christ's cross and that she would receive that cross as well.

Edith was forced to resign her teaching position due to antisemitic laws; she spent long hours in prayer and finally entered the Carmelite order in 1934. Her religious name, Sr. Teresa Benedicta of the Cross, was taken in honor of St. Teresa of Avila, whose autobiography inspired her conversion to Catholicism.

Continued Conversion

Once Sr. Teresa Benedicta settled into life as a Carmelite, her former harsh rigidity started to fade away. She learned, rather clumsily, to perform simple manual housework and became joyful in her obedience. She also began to form a deep connection to the writings of St. John of the Cross.

Thanks to a directive from the provincial of the Carmelite order, Sr. Teresa Benedicta resumed her intellectual work and returned to writing. Her great written work, *Finite and Eternal Being (Enliches und Ewiges Sein)*, was largely composed during the period between her initial and final vows. She took her final vows in 1937.

Shortly after those vows, she was sent to the Netherlands to finish *Finite and Eternal Being* away from the threat of the Nazis. Unfortunately, the book was not published until after her death because she was a Jewish author. Initially, she worked with a small publishing house based in Breslau to try to have the book published. Even that publishing house had to back away during revising and editing due to the intensifying political climate. No other publishing house would even consider the book for fear of Nazi reprisal, and it remained unpublished until 1950.

While in the Netherlands, Sr. Teresa Benedicta also wrote *The Science of the Cross (Kreuzeswissenschaft)*, which was based on the teachings of St. John of the Cross and was to be her final work. It is considered to be roughly written—as her access to research materials at the time she was writing was very limited—as well as somewhat unedited and unpolished. However, it is still thought to contain valuable intellectual observations.

The Nazis invaded the Netherlands in 1940. Sr. Teresa Benedicta remained in the Carmelite convent, where she was safe for a time. In 1942, most of the Christian churches in the Netherlands protested antisemitism and Jewish persecution; the bishops of the Netherlands, as part of this effort, published a letter defending the Jewish people. A few weeks later, most Catholics and other Christians—basically any non-Aryan Christians—were arrested in reprisal.

Sr. Teresa Benedicta and her sister Rosa—who had also become a Carmelite after her conversion—were forced out of her convent and taken away by the Gestapo on August 2, 1942. She was seen a few days later at the Westerbork concentration camp and then sent on to Auschwitz. Sr. Teresa Benedicta was gassed to death at Auschwitz on August 9, 1942.

Her Legacy

Concentration camp survivors who encountered Sr. Teresa Benedicta at Westerbork and during the transit to Auschwitz later reported that she was calm and peaceful. She focused on assisting others at the camp and on the train despite the horrific fate that she almost certainly knew awaited them at the end of the journey. She was beatified in 1987 and canonized as a saint in 1998.

Scholars have pointed out that had Sr. Teresa Benedicta of the Cross, the Carmelite nun, remained Edith Stein, the intellectual, philosopher, and writer, she could have fled to the United States to take refuge from the Nazis' persecution of Jews (Jones, 1999). However, because she was Sr. Teresa Benedicta and had taken a vow of obedience, she stayed in Europe despite the great risk. Her death, then, was truly a sacrifice for her faith. She deeply understood what it meant to abandon herself to the will of God.

Sr. Teresa Benedicta felt that she belonged to God spiritually and bodily, through the duality of her Jewish roots and her Catholic faith. To her, becoming Catholic was not a rejection of her Jewish origin so much as a fulfillment of it.

In fact, her last recorded words to her sister as they were forced out of their convent were, "Come, we are going for our people" (as cited in Coppen, 2022). She saw her death as a sacrifice to be made for the Jewish people, with whom she still identified strongly.

At the time of her canonization, some people protested that the Church was appropriating her death as martyrdom for her Catholic faith, despite the fact that Sr. Teresa Benedicta was killed because of her Jewish heritage. Others worried that her story would spark some Christians to try to force Christianity upon groups of Jewish people.

As Pope John Paul II and the U.S. Bishops' Committee pointed out, though, honoring Sr. Teresa Benedicta allows us to remember and honor all of the Jewish people who were killed by Nazi violence. As the Bishops' Committee put it, "In honoring Edith Stein, the Church wishes to honor all the millions of Jewish victims of the Shoah. Christian veneration of Edith Stein does not lessen but rather strengthens our need to preserve and honor the memory of the Jewish victims" (as cited in Coppen, 2022).

After all, Sr. Teresa Benedicta embraced her Jewish heritage and Catholic beliefs. She offers an example of what is possible when we take a "both/and" approach rather than an "either/or" stance. What's more, she shows us that the life of the mind can be the life of faith, too, when intellectual gifts are put at the service of God.

Sr. Teresa Benedicta's story shows us the tremendous good that can arise when we passionately seek truth—especially when we are willing to become uncomfortable or even confront previous beliefs in search of truth. It took great courage and great commitment to the truth she found for her to turn away from both atheism and Judaism to declare herself a Catholic, knowing that she risked damaging her relationship with her mother and her family.

Yet, even though her conversion and subsequent vocation to religious life in many ways forced Sr. Teresa Benedicta to leave behind everything that was familiar to her, she embraced her newfound faith and allowed herself to be transformed by it. She became more joyful and more humble as she dove more deeply into her vocation.

In addition to her inspiring faith, Sr. Teresa Benedicta also leaves us a rich intellectual heritage. Many of her original writings and German translations of Latin works have now been published, thus sharing her tremendous intellect with a wider audience. Her philosophy has appealed to Catholic and nonreligious scholars for the depth of its observations.

More than anything, Sr. Teresa Benedicta's life demonstrates an unflinching willingness to face suffering and the redemptive power that embracing our crosses can bring. She knew that salvation comes through the cross. It is worth struggling through extremely difficult situations because eternal good can result from them.

Sr Teresa Benedicta spoke with boldness, wrote with boldness, and, above all, clung to her faith with boldness. She lived during a time when it would have been tempting to hide her intellectual gifts and her identity as both Jewish and Catholic, but instead, she embraced them. Her martyrdom helps us remember that God can take a situation designed to destroy and turn it into an instrument of salvation.

Saint Teresa Benedicta of the Cross, pray for us!

Reflection Questions

- Edith's early life was marked by her quest for truth. How has your own search for truth manifested itself in your life?

- Sr. Teresa Benedicta saw her conversion to Catholicism as the fulfillment rather than a rejection of her Jewish heritage, similar to the first Christians. Where do you experience tension between different aspects of your identity? How have you resolved this, if you have?

- No one would have faulted Edith Stein for keeping a low profile or for escaping Nazi Germany, but she did neither. Are there gifts or talents you have or areas of your life you are tempted to hide? Why or why not?

Chapter 6:

Thea Bowman 1937-1990

United States

In History

- The 1954 Supreme Court case of Brown v. Board of Education ended legal racial segregation of public schools in the United States. High schools were to be the first to integrate, and on September 4, 1957, the "Little Rock Nine" attempted to enter Central High School in Little Rock, Arkansas. Federal troops were sent to escort the students into the school.

- The U.S. Civil Rights Act of 1964 was passed to stop employment discrimination on the basis of race, color, sex, religion or national origin.

- White women gained the right to vote in the United States on August 18, 1920 with the ratification of the 19th Amendment, but because of a loophole in the 15th Amendment, women of color were not allowed to vote until the 1965 Voting Rights Act was passed. The Voting Rights Act also removed literacy tests as a precursor to voting, a caveat designed to hinder black and brown voters.

In Society

- The civil rights movement started in the late 1940s and continued until the late 1960s to end racial discrimination and have equal rights under the law for Black Americans. The movement was successful in helping to pass laws to protect American rights regardless of color, race, sex, or national origin.

- In 1957, Martin Luther King, Jr. became the president of the Southern Christian Leadership Conference, which was formed to lead the civil rights movement to gain equal rights for black Americans. King employed Christian ideals and was inspired to use nonviolent methods, as Mahatma Gandhi did in India. In 1963, King delivered his famous "I Have a Dream" speech during the historic March on Washington for Jobs and Freedom.

- Toy manufacturer Mattel introduced Barbie in 1959, a radical departure from the baby dolls that were popular with girls at the time. In 1968 Christie, one of the first black Barbies made, was launched in support of the civil rights movement.

We unite ourselves with Christ's redemptive work when we reconcile, when we make peace, when we share the good news that God is in our lives, when we reflect to our brothers and sisters God's healing, God's forgiveness, God's unconditional love.

–Sr. Thea Bowman

Sister Thea Bowman was a brilliant intellectual and teacher, a beautiful singer, and a dynamic speaker. She made significant contributions to the evangelization of African Americans through her "ministry of joy," and she became a leader calling for intercultural awareness in the church.

Growing Up

Do you know a precocious child? One that makes you think, "I can't wait to see what that child does when they grow up?" That was Sr. Thea Bowman, born Bertha Elizabeth Bowman in 1937 in Yazoo City, Mississippi. The granddaughter of formerly enslaved people, her parents were both highly educated, as she would also become—her mother was a teacher, and her father was a doctor. Her heritage as an African American was of central importance throughout her life.

Her parents' only child, Bertha and her family were Protestant and attended a Methodist church. Her parents greatly valued education and young Bertha attended the Holy Child Jesus School, where she was taught by Franciscan sisters. The sisters inspired her so much that she asked to become Catholic at the tender age of nine years old. Thanks to the example of the sisters, she saw

Catholics as people who loved and cared for each other and for the poor—truly putting their faith into action.

Both before and after her conversion to Catholicism, Bertha enjoyed listening to the older members of her community. From the community elders, she learned survival skills to cope with racism, segregation, and inequality as well as learning about the richness of her African American culture, from stories and songs to prayers, traditions, and customs.

When she was just 15, Bertha left her home in Mississippi to join the Franciscan Sisters of Perpetual Adoration in LaCrosse, Wisconsin. Her parents initially opposed her vocation and forbade her to go; she actually went on a hunger strike in protest. They were worried about how she would be received as an African American both in LaCrosse and in the order.

Bertha soon convinced her parents to let her pursue her vocation; when she arrived in LaCrosse, she was the only African American member of the community and faced reactions ranging from curiosity to outright racism. She took the name Sister Mary Thea in honor of Mary, the Mother of God, and her father Theon. Her name, Thea, literally translates to "God."

Religious Life

As a novice, Sr. Thea was devoted to the Eucharist. She tried to see God's will in any situation she faced. She soon entered Viterbo College to complete her bachelor's degree, training to be a teacher with a particular focus on English and linguistics. Soon after, Sr. Thea returned to Mississippi and spent a few years teaching at Holy Child Jesus School. Then she left Mississippi for the Catholic University of America, where she earned both her master's and doctoral degrees in English. She returned to LaCrosse next where she taught English at Viterbo University. Sr. Thea loved to teach and share her knowledge with others; teaching was one of her strong, defining charisms.

Sr Thea was an active participant in the spiritual and cultural awakening that took place in the U.S. in the 1960s, both in the secular world and in the church after the Second Vatican Council. As a result, she felt called to share her African American cultural heritage with others, especially in the church.

She embraced the rich traditions of her patrimony as an African American, a Southerner, and a descendant of enslaved people—using these identities to share the joy of the Gospel while never shrinking away from her roots. Sr. Thea was a singer, speaker, writer, and evangelizer who drew upon her cultural heritage to spread the message of Christ's love.

Raising Cultural Awareness

After spending quite a few years teaching, Sr Thea moved back to Mississippi to help take care of her aging parents and to work as a consultant for intercultural awareness in the Diocese of Jackson upon the bishop's invitation. In this role, she worked to dismantle cultural barriers between people who were divided by race, class, and other societal identifiers.

Sr Thea encouraged people to communicate with each other and truly learn each other's stories, believing that this was the best way to cross the divides between different races and classes. Her demeanor was extremely joyful and welcoming, and she sought to bring out those same qualities in others. She was known for wearing bright clothing in traditional African patterns and for her rich singing voice.

She was especially committed to sharing African American culture and heritage with children. Sr. Thea used her gift of song to help the children she worked with learn about their identity as a child of God and about their cultural heritage. She used stories, songs, and dance to teach them what it meant to be African American and Catholic.

Sr. Thea was one of the founding members of the Institute for Black Catholic Studies at Xavier University in New Orleans, which held its inaugural courses in 1980. In 1982, the Institute launched its Master's in Pastoral Theology, and Sr. Thea joined the faculty to teach African American Literature and Preaching.

Many African Americans are Protestant, with only about 6% of U.S. Catholics identifying as African American (Pratt, 2022). But Sr. Thea recognized that even though African Americans make up a minority in the U.S. Catholic Church, they have a unique spirituality. She wanted to share that spirituality with the larger Church, and she began to travel around the U.S. and even internationally to minister to African American Catholics.

The year 1984 was difficult on a personal level for Sr. Thea. Both of her parents passed away, and she was diagnosed with breast cancer. Despite the health challenges that she faced, Sr. Thea continued speaking and writing until her death in 1990. She famously prayed to "Live until I die," and she certainly did just that (*Sister Thea Bowman's Story,* n.d.). While she was fighting cancer and eventually confined to a wheelchair, in 1987 alone she still helped to organize the Black Catholic

Congress, appeared on the TV show *60 Minutes,* and contributed to the publication of *Lead Me, Guide Me: The African American Catholic Hymnal.*

Particularly through her music ministry, Sr. Thea pushed for the Church to be a more participatory space: for everyone to join together in worship. She used her own musical gifts—as music was another one of her strong charisms—and her knowledge of African American spirituals as a way of showing what it could look like to be authentically both African American and Catholic. Sr. Thea had grown up surrounded by spiritual music and during her academic studies; she realized just how much music expressed what it meant to be African American.

Importantly, music was also a way of her using cultural heritage to inform her spirituality and worship while still remaining faithful to the Church's theology. Sr. Thea saw the Church as beautifully positioned to help build relationships between people of all races because it is, at once, both universal and local.

Sr. Thea and Education
Sr. Thea also strongly supported Catholic schools and Catholic education, especially for people of African American descent. In fact, Sr. Thea was instrumental in starting the Sister Thea Bowman Black Catholic Education Foundation to offer young, economically underprivileged African Americans a chance to earn a degree from a partnering Catholic college or university. The Foundation also gives its scholars opportunities to explore works of literature and theology that particularly address the African American religious experience. As of this publication, it has helped over 250 students complete their degrees and has a remarkable 98%

retention rate (*Sister Thea Bowman Black Catholic Education Foundation History*, n.d.).

Sr. Thea wrote a book in 1985, *Families Black and Catholic, Catholic and Black*, at the request of the U.S. Conference of Catholic Bishops. Her book was aimed at those who ministered to African American Catholics and was soon widely adopted by various U.S. dioceses.

Boston College granted her an honorary doctorate in 1989 and later named its African, Hispanic, Asian, and Native American (AHANA) and Intercultural Center after her, declaring it the Thea Bowman AHANA and Intercultural Center.

One of Sr. Thea's last major public speeches came in 1989, when she addressed the United States Conference of Catholic Bishops at their annual meeting. She talked to the bishops about what it meant to be both African American and Catholic and encouraged them to evangelize African American communities. She also exhorted them to promote African American participation in the church and attendance at Catholic schools. Most memorably, she finished her talk by asking the bishops to stand and sing "We Shall Overcome"—one of the most notable songs of the Civil Rights movement—with her.

Her Legacy

Sr. Thea posthumously received the Laetare Medal from the University of Notre Dame in 1990, and there are almost 20 institutions around the United States named in her honor—ranging from schools to medical institutions that serve the poor and affordable housing options for the elderly. Yearly, Notre Dame presents a Sr. Thea

Bowman award that honors two students for a commitment to social justice.

The start of her cause for canonization was approved by the U.S. Conference of Catholic Bishops in 2018, and later that year, Sr. Thea was declared a Servant of God.

Sr. Thea, with her proud advocacy for the African American community, boldly proclaimed her cultural heritage. She aimed to express the Church's rich theology within African American culture. She sought to embrace both the history of the church and the history of African Americans and showed that she could be both authentically African American and authentically Catholic.

During her work in the 1970s and 1980s, she carried forward the legacy of the Civil Rights movement in many ways. Sr. Thea encouraged people to be individuals while being one in Christ. She recognized the uniqueness of each person and each culture while also recognizing that as brothers and sisters in Christ, we have more in common than we realize.

Sr. Thea often referred to her work as a *ministry of joy*. She knew that evangelizing was about much more than sermonizing. It involved teaching, building relationships, making connections, and showing people they were loved. Most crucially, she wanted everyone to know that they were loved by God.

She wasn't afraid to challenge people and push them to greater attainments; she also wanted them to be more keenly aware of their own gifts and talents. Sr. Thea knew that the church is at its best when all of its members celebrate and share their gifts.

Instead, Sr. Thea wanted everyone in the church to be free to express their cultural heritage, unique spiritual gifts, and God-given talents so that the church would be richer and fuller. She loved the Catholic Church, and she knew the Catholic Church could provide a place for everyone, particularly for African Americans.

That isn't to say that Sr. Thea thought the Church was perfect; she called out aspects of Church history that were segregationist or racially unjust and engaged in discussions with Church leaders about how to change things in the future. Sr. Thea shows us that we can love the Church and also hold it accountable, and that we can spend our lives promoting our faith while also recognizing aspects that need to change.

Sr. Thea had a huge impact on the Church in the United States, particularly on the way the Church ministers to African Americans. Like so many saints, she focused on doing what God asked of her in the time and place she lived, with perfect openness to His will and with great love. She knew that we all have a responsibility to try to make life better for others.

She could have focused on racial injustice, but Sr Thea chose to be a messenger of joy and an instrument of the Gospel. She refused to let her physical suffering at the end of her life prevent her from fulfilling her mission to travel and share the Gospel. Sr Thea shows us the power of trust and hope, as well as the tremendous joy that can result when we focus on God and try to seek His will every day.

Servant of God Sr. Thea Bowman, pray for us!

Reflection Questions

- Sr. Thea's childhood spent listening to her elders and her identity as an African American both played an important part in her spirituality. How has your spirituality been informed by your ethnicity and/or community?

- Are there under-represented groups in your parish? Could you help create space for them to share their unique gifts?

- Sr. Thea offered her love of music and beautiful singing voice as part of her ministry. How do you share your talents in your parish and/or community?

Chapter 7:

Gianna Beretta Molla 1922-1962

Italy

In History

- Benito Mussolini was an Italian dictator who established the National Fascist Party and coined the term "fascism." He was also the Italian Prime Minister from 1922 until he was deposed in 1943.

- Mussolini's regime sided with Germany at the beginning of World War II, but after a series of military failures, nearly constant internal fighting, and a new government in place in 1943 after Mussolini's removal, Italy joined the Allies in their fight against Nazi Germany.

- German troops poured into northern Italy when the country changed loyalties, while Allied troops landed in ports in southern Italy. This, coupled with pockets of resistance fighting in the north, resulted in fierce, brutal combat in the towns and streets along the entire Italian peninsula as each side tried to gain ground and control. Often, civilians were victims of the fighting, leaving many thousands dead.

In Society

- Italy was devastated after World War II, with major portions of ports, railroads, and industrial factories and centers destroyed. There was a significant lack of commodities and high inflation.

- There was also societal tension between those who had supported fascism and those who had not, as well as between many men who had fought in the war and wanted their jobs back and the women who had gone to work while they were gone.

- This period of time gave birth to an artistic movement called neo-realism, in which the lives of the poor and struggling were depicted in Italian films, literature, and art.

Love is the most beautiful sentiment that the Lord has put into the souls of men and women.

–Gianna Beretta Molla

A successful physician, wife, and mother of four, during Gianna Beretta Molla's last pregnancy, a tumor was found that threatened both her and the baby's lives. True to her belief in the sanctity of life, she opted to save the baby's life and died of complications after her daughter was born.

Early Life

Do you come from a small or a large family? Imagine being the tenth child out of thirteen. Well, in 1922, in Magenta, Italy, Gianna Beretta was born as the tenth child to her already large family, although, five of her siblings died in infancy or early childhood. Her fervently Catholic and pious family was led by both of her parents, who valued education and saw it their duty to educate their children as the work of God, especially as Third Order Franciscans.

The family moved to Bergamo when Gianna was three and then to Genoa when she was five. The Beretta home was peaceful and joyful. The family lived simply, and Gianna's parents encouraged generosity and sacrifice. Gianna attended Mass daily from a very young age. She also prayed the Rosary daily and developed a deep prayer life.

While a student, Gianna became a member of Catholic Action—a lay movement still active today that seeks to intensify the spiritual life of members of the laity and thus inspire them to further apostolic and charitable work. The Catholic Action motto is "prayer, action, sacrifice," and in many respects, this also became the motto for Gianna's life.

Her childhood was not completely idyllic, though; Gianna's older sister, Amelia, to whom she was quite devoted, died in 1937 at the age of 26. This was Gianna's first major experience with suffering. Rather than raging against God, she retreated into a deeper prayer life and later shared that she felt her suffering brought her closer to God and strengthened her faith.

In 1938, Gianna went on a retreat organized by the sisters who ran her school. There, she undertook the Ignatian Spiritual Exercises, an experience that influenced the rest of her life. She resolved to do all things for God according to His will.

When Gianna was only 20 years old, she lost both of her parents in the same year. After their deaths, she decided to study medicine. Gianna was intelligent but had been a fairly mediocre student up to that point, and she had to work very hard on her studies. Following her parents' deaths, she redoubled her efforts and slowly started to thrive at her schoolwork.

She began studying medicine at the University of Pavia in 1942, although she couldn't always attend class because it was wartime and bombings were common. However, she persevered with her studies and eventually graduated with a medical degree in 1949.

During her time at the university, she remained active in the Catholic Action movement. Given the effects of World War II, Gianna organized retreats and other events for the younger members as much as she could.

She became something of a role model for many of the girls that she worked with.

In addition to Catholic Action, Gianna was also a St. Vincent de Paul Society member. Outside of her evangelizing efforts, she was also an avid skier and enjoyed mountain climbing. She was quite devoted to her work for the Church and to living an active life!

The Next Phase of Life

Gianna opened a medical clinic near her hometown of Magenta in 1950 after her graduation. She also continued her studies at the University of Milan from 1950 through 1952, earning a specialization in pediatrics. In her medical practice she was especially drawn to serve mothers and their babies, the elderly, and the poor. Gianna was known to treat people even if she knew they couldn't pay, and she had a special charism for walking with mothers facing difficult pregnancies (whether physically or emotionally).

Her brother was a priest who did missionary work in Brazil, and she strongly considered joining him as a lay missionary to use her medical training to help poor women. She saw practicing medicine as a mission, not just a job. Ultimately, various complications with paperwork as well as a realization that her health may not be strong enough to undergo missionary work kept Gianna in Italy.

She went on a pilgrimage to Lourdes in 1954 with the goal of discerning God's will for her life, whether that was religious life or marriage. The constant obstacles she met while attempting to explore a calling as a lay missionary caused her to doubt the direction of God's plan for her life, and she spent hours in deep prayer while on pilgrimage.

Ultimately, she discerned that God was calling her to a vocation of marriage. Shortly after her trip to Lourdes, Gianna met Pietro Molla, an engineer. They were engaged in 1955, just a few months after they met, and then married a few months later. Gianna's brother celebrated their wedding mass, and she carefully chose the material for her dress with the dream that one day, her wedding dress would be reused as a chasuble for one of her sons. (Fittingly, the Society of Saint Gianna obtained a small piece of her wedding dress from Pietro and incorporated it into a chasuble that is often used by priests celebrating Mass at the St. Gianna Shrine in Warminster, Pennsylvania.)

Pietro and Gianna's first child, Pierluigi, was born in 1956, and their second child, Maria Zita, followed in 1957. Their third child, Laura, was born in 1959. Although Gianna suffered from hyperemesis (constant vomiting) during all of her pregnancies, she retained her peaceful, joyful attitude and continued to rely on God to sustain her.

Gianna kept practicing medicine after her marriage and the births of their children; she was also devoted to her children and to her husband. By all accounts, their family life was quite happy and deeply spiritual—imitating the type of home she'd grown up in as a child.

Gianna, along with Pietro, continued to enjoy ski trips and time in the mountains. They attended the symphony and the opera, and she dabbled in painting. Gianna also loved fine clothing. She always chose modest styles that she described as having simple elegance.

Her Fourth Pregnancy

Gianna experienced two miscarriages before becoming pregnant with their fourth child in 1961. But only two months into the pregnancy, she experienced intense pain and was diagnosed with a noncancerous uterine fibroid. She was given the choice of a hysterectomy—which would remove both the fibroid and the uterus with the growing baby—an abortion along with removal of the fibroid, or removal of the fibroid only.

She decided, without question, that surgery should remove only the uterine fibroid, even though her doctors counseled that this was the riskiest option for her. Gianna, as a doctor herself, understood the medical situation clearly and was quite adamant in her instructions that every effort should be made to leave her uterus intact and keep the child safe.

The remainder of the pregnancy, like her previous pregnancies, was quite difficult, but Gianna remained dedicated to her vocation as a mother and a doctor despite the physical discomfort that she faced. She kept seeing patients until just a short time before the baby was born.

Their daughter Gianna Emanuela Molla was born via C-section in April 1962. Soon after her daughter's birth, Gianna developed peritonitis from postoperative complications. She was in extreme pain but refused painkillers because she didn't like how they made her feel. She died just a week after Gianna Emanuela's birth due to the peritonitis.

Amazingly, Gianna seemingly had a hunch that she would not survive long after the birth of her baby. She told her husband several times that if he had to make a choice between saving the baby's life or saving her life, he should choose the baby without thinking. During her last few days of life, she repeated the words "Jesus, I love you" over and over (*St. Gianna's Life*, n.d.).

Her Legacy

Gianna was beatified in 1994—appropriately, during the Year of the Family. She was later canonized in 2004. Pietro and their children were present at her canonization: This was the first time in Church history that a husband was a witness to his wife's canonization. St. Gianna was also the first female physician to be canonized. She is the patroness of mothers, physicians, and unborn children. Since her canonization, St. Gianna has become the inspiration and namesake for many, many pro-life centers and pro-life organizations around the world.

When first reading her story, the thing that jumps out to most people is her heroic choice to keep her baby safe despite knowing that it was a riskier option for her own health. But in many ways, St. Gianna's whole life prepared her to make that choice. She made small choices each day that added up to a life of heroic virtue.

She chose to prioritize Mass and prayer on a daily basis, and she chose to offer everything she did to the will of God. St. Gianna had a deep, fundamental trust in God and surrendered herself completely to His will. Her heroic virtue was formed not in one dramatic moment, but through a lifetime of small choices to say yes to God.

St. Gianna also shows us the importance of creating a family dynamic that prioritizes forming children in Christian values. She grew up in this type of home and then created a similar environment in which to raise her own children, and it became a breeding ground for saintliness. Joy, peace, generosity, and deep trust in God were ingrained in her from the start of her life and permeated her entire outlook on life.

But while St. Gianna radiated holiness, she also lived in a way that is accessible to women today. She took care of her children, went to work, and spent time with her husband.

In fact, one of the most appealing and most relatable things about St. Gianna is her "normalcy." She loved skiing and hiking in the mountains, appreciated good clothing, and was passionate about her career. That's a description that likely doesn't sound too far off from someone we know or maybe even ourselves. St. Gianna shows us that we can continue to enjoy our lives while we work toward holiness. Virtue can grow through work, hobbies, and appreciation of beauty just as it can grow through prayer and almsgiving.

She's also a relatable role model for working mothers, as St. Gianna balanced her dedication to her family with her work as a doctor. She loved her children deeply and was very intentional about creating a strong family bond but she also enjoyed her work and was dedicated to her patients.

She was able to balance being a physician, wife, and mother without letting one aspect eclipse the others. St. Gianna shows both that we don't stop being who we were before once we are married and also that we can't let our profession overshadow the needs of our families. Rather, God calls us to find a balance between growing in the talents He gave us and serving the needs of others.

Most importantly, St. Gianna illustrates the sacrificial nature of love. She loved her life, but she loved her baby's life more. Many reflections on her canonization focus on the ultimate sacrifice that she made; however, as a wife and mother, she made many small sacrifices on a daily basis because of her love for her family. She was able to make those small sacrifices with joy due to her submission to God and the promise she had made as a teenager to do everything in accordance with His will.

She saw *life* as a vocation that she was called to do well, and that vocation as a gift from God. As a wife and mother, St. Gianna is a witness to the sanctity of the call to marriage. She had a faithful commitment to her husband and their family. Many more of us are called to marriage than to the consecrated religious life, and women like St. Gianna help us to remember that sainthood can come through children and chaos just as readily as it can come through the convent!

Saint Gianna Beretta Molla, pray for us!

Reflection Questions

- As a working mother, St. Gianna had many demands on her time, as do many of us today. How do you prioritize your responsibilities? Do you still make time for prayer?

- What is the atmosphere in your home? Are there ways you could help it become more conducive to living a holy life?

- St. Thérèse of Lisieux wrote about her "Little Way," offering small sacrifices in our daily lives to God. Similarly, St. Gianna's life prepared her to choose to save her fourth baby. What aspects of your daily life can you offer to God to grow in holiness?

Chapter 8:

Cory Aquino 1933-2009

Philippines

In History

- World War II left the Philippines devastated, particularly the capital city Manila, as allied forces successfully ousted the occupying Japanese military. Considerable portions of the country's infrastructure lay in ruins, and its economy as a consequence.

- To gain rehabilitation aid, the newly established Filipino government accepted heavy terms from the United States, including 99-year leases on military and naval bases in the country.

- The Philippine - U.S. relationship was a major focus in Filipino politics for decades after the war, with factions on both sides - those who were pro-American and others who desired more independence for the country.

In Society

- While many people lived in rural, agricultural areas of the Philippines, after World War II there was significant migration to cities, creating some very densely populated areas. The capital city of Manila became especially crowded.

- During the colonial period, a school system was established under the United States to bring education to the masses. Up until then, formal schooling was only for the elite.

- The Philippines claims to be the only Christian country in Asia. The majority of the population, 86%, is Catholic, with another 8% identifying with other Christian denominations. There is also a strong Islamic minority, around 4%, with the remaining 2% of the population identifying with other beliefs.

Faith is not simply a patience that passively suffers until the storm is past. Rather, it is a spirit that bears things— with resignations, yes, but above all, with blazing, serene hope.

–Cory Aquino

Cory Aquino is as well-known as some of the other women chronicled here, yet her fame is based on her political stature as the first female president of the Philippines. What's equally important to highlight is that Cory relied on her Catholic faith to sustain her through the challenges she faced before and after her presidential election.

Early Life

Cory was born Maria Corazon Cojuangco in 1933 in the town of Paniqui, about 40 miles north of Manila. Her family called her by her middle name, Corazon, from the start and soon shortened that to Cory. Her family lineage was Chinese and Spanish, and her parents were wealthy landowners. The Cojuangco family had a comfortable life.

Cory's parents emphasized the Benedictine motto, *Ora et Labora:* Pray and work. Cory sought to embody this; she took her faith seriously and worked hard at her studies. She was always at or near the top of her class in school.

The family moved to Manila soon after Cory was born to be near top Catholic schools for the older children—Cory had seven siblings, although two of them died very young. Despite the family's wealth, the Cojuangco children learned the value of money, and the family lived fairly simply. Their parents strongly emphasized being well-rounded citizens and contributing to Filipino society.

During Cory's childhood, the Philippines was a commonwealth of the United States, though it aimed to become independent. But during World War II, Manila was abandoned to the Japanese while the U.S. focused its resources on other areas of the war. A group of Filipino leaders collaborated with the Japanese to form a new Republic of the Philippines; this group included Cory's father, who became a congressman, and her future father-in-law, Benigno Aquino Sr., who became the Speaker of the National Assembly.

Soon, the U.S. tried to win back the Philippines. Manila was bombarded with bombs and air raids throughout 1945, and Cory's family home was burned. After the U.S. regained control, the Philippines was declared an independent republic in 1946, according to the previous plan. However, the city of Manila and the Filipino economy were in ruins, and there were pockets of guerrillas all over the country—whether advocating for Communism, protesting U.S. involvement in the Philippines, protesting the previous collaboration with Japan, or with any number of other motivations.

Due to the highly unsettled state of the Philippines, the Cojuangco family moved to the United States for several years until things calmed down. Cory finished high school in New York City and, along with her sister, attended the College of Mount St. Vincent in the Bronx. She and her sister were very close, but Cory was otherwise a loner.

She spent summers in the Philippines with her family and reconnected with Benigno Aquino Jr., known as Ninoy; they had known each other as children. She and Ninoy started writing to each other while she finished her degree in French and mathematics at the College of Mount St. Vincent.

Cory returned to the Philippines after graduating from college. The country was more stable then, and she started law school at Far Eastern University. She planned to get involved in the Cojuangco family business.

Meanwhile, her friendship with Ninoy Aquino deepened. He was friends with the Philippine president, Magsaysay, and wanted to get involved in politics. In 1954, the couple told their parents they were thinking about getting married. Their families approved so heartily that Cory and Ninoy made their wedding plans in a rush. They were married just 10 days later, on Cory's parents' wedding anniversary, at Our Lady of the Sorrows Church.

The Life of a Family in Politics

Cory and Ninoy honeymooned in the United States before moving to the Filipino province of Tarlac. Ninoy was soon elected mayor of their town, Concepcion, and became one of the youngest mayors in the Philippines. Thanks to his friendship with President Magsaysay, Ninoy's political career appeared to be on the rise.

Magsaysay remained on friendly terms with the US, which placated many Filipinos, and started various programs to promote economic equality, appeasing other Filipinos, including the Communists. But just when things were looking hopeful for the Philippines, Magsaysay was killed in a plane crash in 1957. Ninoy supported his vice-president, a man named Carlos Garcia, who was soon elected President for a full term. However, Ninoy also had ties to the opposing political party. Due to his political connections, Ninoy became the youngest governor in the Philippines when he was elected Governor of Tarlac Province in 1961.

The Aquino home was regularly full of political leaders, but Cory largely remained in the background during this time. She cared for the couple's five children and listened a lot. Later, she'd share her thoughts about what she had heard with Ninoy. However, her direct involvement in politics did not begin until the 1980s, after Ninoy's death.

To truly understand the significance of Cory's later election as President, it's important to understand the context of the Philippines at that time in addition to learning Cory's own story. The Philippines was full of unrest in the early 1960s, largely due to economic issues. Almost all of the country's wealth was concentrated in the hands of a few, and many Filipinos lived in abject poverty. There were guerillas who strongly advocated for the Philippines to become Communist—and this was at a time when most Western countries, including the US, were highly vigilant to the threat of Communism and formerly democratic countries becoming Communist.

Against this backdrop, Ninoy was elected to the Senate in 1965. During this same election, Ferdinand Marcos became president. Marcos started many programs to foster a sense of nationalism, protect Filipino culture, and try to help the economy, but there was still a huge gap between the rich and the poor, and many opponents accused Marcos of using the presidency to line his own pockets.

Heavy protests during Marcos's second term as president in the late 1960s and early 1970s culminated in a protest by taxi drivers due to an increase in the cost of gas in 1971: a protest that soon became violent. Marcos warned that he would impose martial law if things didn't calm down; his detractors realized that the violent riots would be an easy excuse for Marcos to seize more power for himself.

Ninoy was part of the Liberal party, which opposed Marcos's threat of martial law. Further problems in 1972, including natural disasters and continued economic unrest, did nothing to improve the situation, and Marcos finally declared martial law in September of 1972. He jailed many of his political rivals, including Ninoy.

When Ninoy was jailed, Cory drew strength from her faith. She took their infant daughter and visited prison camps all over the Philippines trying to find out where Ninoy had been imprisoned. It took her 43 days to finally find him. Once she knew where Ninoy was, Cory worked to get him released.

Although Ninoy had not been particularly invested in religion up to this point, he saw a vision of the Blessed Virgin while he was in jail. It affected him deeply, and he realized that Cory's faith might be more important than he had realized. Together, they accepted their suffering patiently but also acted to alleviate it. Slowly, Cory was able to win concessions that improved Ninoy's prison conditions and allowed them to visit more often and for longer periods.

Martial Law in the Philippines

Marcos set up a new constitution after declaring martial law, and Cory and Ninoy worked together to fight it. She was his eyes, ears, and voice outside of the jail. They partnered with attorneys and other Marcos opponents to sue the government and declare the new constitution illegal, but they lost. However, Cory and Ninoy kept working to fight against Marcos's regime and secure Ninoy's freedom.

For two years, Cory called regular press conferences to bring attention to Ninoy's situation. He was finally brought to trial in 1977 and sentenced to death. After the trial, Ninoy went on a hunger strike; Cory brought him liquid vitamins and tried to keep his strength up. He was eventually hospitalized 40 days into the hunger strike, and Marcos was forced to temporarily revoke the execution order due to Ninoy's poor health.

The family was eventually allowed to sometimes spend the night together in Ninoy's jail cell at Fort Bonifacio. As their children all slept together on the cold cell floor, Cory and Ninoy's eyes were opened to the lives of the poor and what they had to prioritize: food, shelter, and medicine for their children. Cory and Ninoy realized that for the Filipinos living in terrible poverty, keeping their families alive and sheltered was much more important than the type of government in power. This was a realization that would serve Cory well in later years.

Meanwhile, the U.S. was increasingly bothered by the criticism of Marcos's policies from many Filipinos and reports that Marcos was violating human rights. The

Archbishop of Manila was also extremely critical of the imposed martial law.

Cory was outspoken about Ninoy's poor health and weak heart, and thanks to all of the publicity, Ninoy was finally allowed to return home on house arrest for a month at the end of 1979. But he needed triple bypass surgery. The family was granted permission to travel to the U.S. in 1980 so that top surgeons could perform the surgery. Afterward, they stayed in the U.S.

They moved to Boston, where Ninoy became a research fellow at MIT and Harvard. He closely followed international global affairs and the situation in the Philippines. Protests against Marcos's tactics continued. Cardinal Jaime Sin, the archbishop of Manila, was especially critical.

Ninoy, through Cory, had sent Marcos a proposal in 1979, in which he outlined a three-year plan that would lead to the end of martial law. Now, from the US, he sent Marcos some ideas in an attempt to convince him to step down as leader of the Philippines. Ninoy planned to return to the Philippines at the end of 1982 to persuade Marcos in person.

But Marcos's wife, Imelda, was visiting New York City. She met with Ninoy and warned him to stay away. She offered him a position in business with a comfortable salary if he stepped out of politics.

Ninoy was so angry about Imelda's bribe that he formed his own political party, which he christened *Laban*. Soon after forming Laban, Ninoy's previously suspended death sentence was confirmed; he was warned that if he returned to the Philippines, he would be arrested.

But despite the threat of arrest as well as reported plots to murder him, Ninoy decided to return home to the Philippines anyway. He donned a bulletproof vest before debarking his plane, but he was tragically assassinated by a shot to the head almost immediately after exiting the aircraft.

Cory was devastated but presented a strong face to the public. Almost two million people participated in Ninoy's funeral rites, and people all over the Philippines called for Cory to take her husband's place in politics. The situation in the Philippines was worsening, with mass demonstrations in the streets almost daily.

Becoming a Politician

There was a widespread expectation that Marcos would be forced to call an open presidential election by the end of 1985. Many people suggested that Cory Aquino was the only person with enough political savvy to rise far enough above political differences to be able to unite the people and defeat Marcos.

Cory herself finally agreed that if there were an election, she would run... if over a million people signed a petition to support her candidacy. Near the end of 1985, Marcos finally called a snap election, which would take place in February 1986. The petition for Cory to run for president had over one million signatures within a month.

Cory knew that if she was going to win the election, she'd need support not just from the rich and the political elite but from the poor of the Philippines. Voting fraud was a huge problem, and Marcos was well-known for buying votes, stuffing ballot boxes, and preventing his opposition from voting. He spent huge sums of money paying the poor for their votes.

So, Cory prayed and asked God to show her what to do. After receiving counsel from a priest, she realized that she had to present herself as the opposite of Marcos: that he was a symbol of evil and suffering, and she was a symbol of light. She had to show the people that she was a victim of Marcos, and they were, too.

Cory asked an old family friend and savvy politician in his own right, Salvador Laurel, to run with her as the vice president. When the election date rolled around, voter fraud was a huge problem, just as everyone had expected. The voting totals on the results posted—showing Marcos as the winner—often didn't match when compared to the totals that voting centers had submitted; this escalated to the point where many clerks resigned in protest. The voter fraud had been so outrageous that even the Catholic Bishops Conference issued a statement against it. Despite the obvious corruption, the National Assembly eventually declared Marcos the winner.

Cory was certain that she would be the winner if an accurate count were made. She held a rally in Manila to launch nonviolent boycotts against Marcos and his political associates. The tide began to turn when, shockingly, the Defense Minister, Juan Ponce Enrile, and the Deputy Chief of Staff of the Armed Forces, Fidel Ramos, both announced that they no longer supported Marcos and called for his resignation so that the rightfully elected president could take office. Enrile had helped keep Ninoy in prison years earlier, so Cory was especially surprised by his support.

In retaliation, Marcos ordered combat units to move against Enrile, Ramos, and Cory's other supporters. But thousands of Filipinos knelt in the streets, praying silently, and prevented Marcos's tanks from advancing. Enrile and Ramos declared a new provisional government with Cory as the leader, and Marcos's other officials began resigning. The Marcos regime was collapsing from within.

The First Female President of the Philippines

Cory was inaugurated as President on February 25, 1986, as Marcos and his family fled to the U.S. Cory started putting together her government, a mix of former Marcos supporters and longtime opponents. She faced an incredibly challenging situation: a poor economy and a stringently divided populace.

Cory worried about what to do, and she prayed for guidance. The time she spent in prayer gave her the confidence to do what was in her capacity and leave the rest to God.

It wasn't long before Enrile began to criticize Cory and her administration openly. She traveled to the U.S. to ask for aid; although Congress denied her request, she was well-received, and the publicity surrounding her trip was highly complementary. While in Washington, D.C., Cory visited the Shrine of the Immaculate Conception and was able to pray there.

After returning to the Philippines, she put together a new constitution and scheduled a vote for the people to approve it in February 1987. Enrile continued to undermine her ideas and her work until he finally was caught going too far and planning a coup. Cory asked for his resignation at the end of 1986. While her supporters praised her strong stance and she worked with local Communist leaders to agree to a period of peace, there were continued protests from her political opponents.

Marcos reportedly was planning to return to the Philippines until he was foiled by American authorities and prevented from leaving the US. Land reform also continued to be a hot-button issue. Regardless, Cory's new constitution was approved by a huge majority during the February election, and importantly, the election was peaceful.

When Cory was asked how she envisioned her government—pro-U.S. or pro-Communist—she answered that she envisioned a pro-Filipino government. She served one six-year term, from 1986 until 1992, despite at least six plots to overthrow her. Fidel Ramos, who had served as her Defense Secretary, succeeded her. After her term as President ended, Cory continued to speak out about the Filipino people's challenges. She was particularly vocal against government policies that she saw as threatening democracy and helped lead a think tank on nonviolence.

Cory helped her son campaign for the Senate in 2007, but she was diagnosed with colon cancer and passed away in 2009, just a month before he was elected President of the Philippines.

Her Legacy

Cory was named "Woman of the Year" by TIME Magazine in 1986 and is a tremendously important figure in Filipino history. However, Cory's impact is not just limited to her political contributions. Above all, she was a woman of faith who believed everything happened as God intended. She once commented that prayers are often answered in unforeseen ways; her life certainly gives witness to that statement. The prayers that she and Ninoy had once offered for their beloved Philippines to return to democracy were answered not by his election to the presidency but by hers.

Cory's faith in the will of God also helped her to overcome suffering, anguish, and grief, particularly when Ninoy was imprisoned and again after his assassination. By seeking to discern God's will for her in the midst of her suffering, Cory was able to make sense of the tragedies that her family faced. She relied heavily on prayer. Cory said that prayer clarified her thoughts and helped her navigate her many challenges.

As a woman of faith, Cory had the inner strength that she needed to oppose Ferdinand Marcos and lead the Philippines back to democracy. Her faith shaped who she was, and she, in turn, helped shape the Philippines. She never set out to be a politician who changed the world, but when she was thrust into that role, she trusted that it was all part of the plan that God intended, and she trusted Him to lead her way.

Cory Aquino, pray for us!

Reflection Questions

- After her husband's assassination, Cory was able to take on a political career thanks to the many years she had supported his efforts. Consider the huge responsibility Cory had in taking on this new role. How do you imagine she felt? How would you find the strength to do this very thing?

- Cory did not expect to become a politician like her husband and was reluctant to run for president. In what areas do you struggle to accept God's plan for your life?

- Cory prayed and sought guidance from trusted clergy in her political decision making. How do you bring your faith into your work?

Chapter 9:
Mary Evaline Wolff
(Sr. M. Madeleva Wolff) 1887-1964
United States

In History

- The United States began the 1900s with 45 states. The last states in the lower 48, New Mexico, Arizona, and Oklahoma, all joined the Union by 1912. Alaska and Hawaii did not become states until 1959.

- In 1900, 60% of U.S. high school diplomas were awarded to women since many men entered the workforce during their teens. However, higher education was still largely reserved for men, with only 19% of bachelor's degrees going to women that same year, increasing briefly to 40% by 1930. The percentage of women students fluctuated for much of the 20th century. It was not until the 1970s that women earning college degrees reached pre-World War II levels, arriving at parity with men in the early 1980s.

- Gender discrimination in educational settings was prohibited in the United States with the passage of Title IX in 1972. This legislation created opportunities for women in both sports and academia and brought about a nationwide increase in female enrollment at universities.

In Society

- The number of 20th-century American women becoming nuns increased yearly until it peaked in the mid-1960s, when there were more than 180,000 nuns in the United States. Since then, the number of religious women has declined each year.

- The age of mass media was ushered in by technological advancements in printing in the early 20th century. These advancements made it possible for the first time to produce paperback books and greeting cards, as well as large quantities of newspapers and magazines. This, coupled with the dawn of advertising from companies like Coca-Cola, made it possible to sell publications affordably and reach millions of people.

- Improvements in the technology used in cinema also contributed to the rise and influence of mass media. The Jazz Singer, released on October 6, 1927, by Warner Bros., was the first movie to include recorded dialogue with the film. Audiences were stunned to hear the actors' voices with the film.

The best qualifications I brought to my office were these: my ability to dream, my capacity to work.

–Sr. M. Madeleva Wolff

Do you have a favorite poet? Anyone from the last century? As a writer and poet, teacher, college administrator, pioneering intellectual and religious sister, Sr. Mary Madeleva Wolff was possibly the most famous nun in the United States in the years prior to Vatican II. She held that "college is a profound part of life, not simply a prelude to it," and she pushed the door for advanced theological studies for women wide open and changed the face of Catholicism along the way.

Early Life

The daughter of hard-working immigrants, Mary Evaline Wolff in 1887 in Wisconsin and known as Eva to her family. Her father had come from Germany and made leather harnesses for teams of horses used for logging. Her mother, the daughter of immigrants, was a farm girl. But despite their own humble occupations, Eva's parents highly valued education and encouraged their children's academic progress.

Eva loved to read. She and her two brothers all attended the University of Wisconsin after graduating from the local public high school. After her first year at the University of Wisconsin, where she studied mathematics, Eva was accepted by Saint Mary's College at Notre Dame in Indiana—a Catholic women's college run by the Sisters of the Holy Cross.

At Saint Mary's, Eva was initially seen as a bit of an independent spirit and sometimes even skipped class. She learned "refinement" and "culture" from some of her wealthier classmates and came to appreciate beautiful clothing and popular fashions. Soon after arriving at Saint Mary's, she also fell in love with Catholic literature and poetry.

The experiences she had on a religious retreat made Eva realize that she wanted to become a Sister of the Holy Cross. She pursued her vocation in earnest after her second year at Saint Mary's and entered the congregation in 1908 at the age of 21. She took the name Sister Mary Madeleva upon professing her first vows. Sr. M. Madeleva made her final vows in 1910 and almost immediately began teaching.

Education on Both Sides of the Teacher's Desk

Sr. M. Madeleva taught high school first and then spent some time teaching at the university. She continued her own education after taking her vows. Not content with the bachelor's degree she had earned from Saint Mary's College in 1909, she next earned a master's degree from Notre Dame in 1918.

Sr. M. Madeleva then spent time in the western U.S. as the principal of schools in Utah and California before studying at the University of California, Berkeley. She earned her PhD from Berkeley in 1925, then did postgraduate work at Oxford University in England— where she studied alongside noted writers like J.R.R. Tolkien and C.S. Lewis. Sr. M. Madeleva was also a correspondent of Thomas Merton. To say that she rubbed elbows with some of the leading Christian authors of her era is an understatement!

After completing her postgraduate work, Sr. M. Madeleva was the founding president of St. Mary of the Wasatch College in Salt Lake City, Utah for eight years. She was then offered the position of president of Saint Mary's College in Indiana in 1934—a position she would hold for the next 27 years.

The Pioneer

Sr. M. Madeleva's views on women and the education of women may not seem extraordinary now, but they were somewhat radical for her time. She believed that when women were educated alongside other women and as *women*, it allowed their education to become their own— whereas when women were educated alongside men, they received a man's education that was not tailored to uniquely feminine strengths. Sr. M. Madeleva strongly believed in the complementarity of men and women.

Her view on the need for education for women, coupled with the complementary natures of men and women, gave rise to her calls for an expanded role of women in both society and the church. Sr. M. Madeleva heavily promoted women's access to a strong education and the need for women to be active, valued participants in society because of the unique perspective they could offer.

One critical aspect of her views about education was Sr. M. Madeleva's idea of where the college curriculum should focus. She felt that there should be a central focus on theology. Sr. M. Madeleva astutely pointed out that religious sisters all over the U.S. were providing religious education, but there was nowhere for them to actually study theology.

With the support of the National Catholic Educational Association, Sr. M. Madeleva contacted Catholic universities with theology programs to inquire about admitting women into their programs. Every school that she reached out to—Notre Dame University, St. Louis University, DePaul University, and the Catholic University of America—turned her down.

Sr. M. Madeleva was not to be deterred. With her bishop's approval, she put a plan in place to establish a School of Sacred Theology at Saint Mary's. She recruited priests to join the faculty and won approval from Rome. The School officially opened in 1943 and granted advanced degrees in Catholic theology to women—both consecrated religious and those in the laity—and laymen.

The School of Sacred Theology continued to train women in theology until 1970, when it closed due to its own success. By that time, women trained at the School had begun teaching theology both at the School and elsewhere, and other theology programs—including the ones that had initially rejected Sr. M. Madeleva's inquiries about admitting women to their programs—began accepting women. During its existence, the School of Sacred Theology produced over 375 graduates, with over 70 of those graduating with a PhD and over 300 with a master's degree.

Establishing the School of Sacred Theology wasn't the only accomplishment of Sr. M. Madeleva's tenure as president of Saint Mary's. Under her guidance, the school became a center of contemporary Catholic thought. She brought in Catholic writers, thinkers, performers, and artists to expose the students to art and literature.

Moreover, Sr. M. Madeleva welcomed international students to campus. At one point, students from over 38 different countries studied at Saint Mary's College. She was also in favor of ecumenism long before the focus on this in Vatican II.

Her most controversial decision as president, though, was probably her decision to integrate campus in 1941 and welcome the first African American students. Sr. M. Madeleva waved off her critics and justified the need for integration based on the teachings of the Gospel.

In addition to her efforts at Saint Mary's, Sr. M. Madeleva played a huge role in improving professional training for all religious sisters, no matter where they studied. At the National Catholic Education Association's meeting in 1949, Sr. M. Madeleva began campaigning for better training and easier access to education for religious sisters. She pointed out that they taught the huge majority of the students in Catholic schools across the country yet received a limited, fragmented collegiate education themselves in most cases.

For the next several years, Sr. M. Madeleva was instrumental in putting together the Sister Formation Movement. The first Sister Formation Conference was held in 1952. The group focused on preparing incoming sisters and giving them proper, professional training and a quality education before sending them to Catholic schools to teach.

The Poet and Author

If all of her efforts in the academic world weren't enough, Sr. M. Madeleva balanced all of this with her own prolific writing career. She was a consistent poet, producing approximately a poem a month for a period spanning over a decade, and she had her poems accepted by publications like The New Republic, Commonweal, and The New York Times.

Over the course of her lifetime, Sr. M. Madeleva published over 20 books, and 13 of those were volumes of poetry. Her most famous poem was probably *Snow Storm*, which was featured in the 1939 World's Fair in New York City. She was also the president of the Catholic Poetry Society of America for a period of time.

Hallmark featured some of her verses on their greeting cards, and when Boston College ran the David B. Steinman Visiting Poets Series in 1957 and 1958, Sr. M. Madeleva was the only female poet invited to speak. The roster included other such noteworthy, contemporary mid-century poets as Robert Frost, Ogden Nash, and T.S. Eliot.

Sr. M. Madeleva was the president of Saint Mary's College until 1961. During her tenure, the school saw its enrollment nearly triple. She died in 1964 of septicemia after undergoing surgery.

Her Legacy

As one biographer put it, Sr. M. Madeleva had the unique ability of "cherishing tradition without clinging to it" (Mandell, 2010, p. 92). She embraced the Church's theology while also recognizing that the methods for sharing that theology needed updating. Her influence on Catholic education in the United States is undeniable.

Because of Sr. M. Madeleva, religious sisters who teach are now undoubtedly better formed, better educated, and better prepared in both their pedagogy and their foundational knowledge. She was a strong advocate for women's education, whether the woman in question was heading for the convent or heading for a lay vocation. Her ideas about educating women and, specifically, about the educational needs of religious sisters had a far-reaching impact on Catholic universities.

Without Sr. M. Madeleva, it's hard to tell what the evolution of advanced theological education for women might look like. Her work to establish the School of Sacred Theology at Saint Mary's had huge repercussions, not just for the women who studied there but also for theological studies in the U.S. as a whole. The women that the School educated would go on to become teachers of other theologians, subtly changing the face of theological study completely.

Sr. M. Madeleva wasn't afraid to make controversial decisions or tackle tough projects. Whether it was integration, forming new academic programs, or revising the way formation was thought of, she was up for the challenge. She put her faith in the Lord and then put herself to work.

Sr. M. Madeleva shows us how the life of faith is often one of practicality and work, in addition to prayer and reflection. As a religious sister, she went out and spread the joy of Christ to the Church and the world. She fulfilled her vocation by dedicating herself to the Lord's work—with a capital W in *Work*!

In addition, Sr. M. Madeleva was one of the first religious sisters to consistently publish her poetry in secular publications and achieve public popularity for her poems. She helped religious orders to see poetry as a worthwhile pursuit and as a facet of one's spiritual identity.

To Sr. M. Madeleva, poetry was a form of prayer. She saw her poems as a way of expressing her relationship with God. Poetry represented divine inspiration, and writing poetry was a way of recognizing God's beauty and giving some of that beauty back to Him.

She shows us that prayer can take many forms and that exercising our creative gifts can, in fact, be a form of prayer. By sharing her poetry in both secular and spiritual publications, Sr. M. Madeleva evangelized the truth and beauty of His creation to people far and wide.

Sr. M. Madeleva's life reminds us that when we put our gifts into God's hands, He may choose to use them in unexpected ways—even in ways that challenge current conventional thought. By submitting our gifts to His service and prayerfully discerning His will, He may use those gifts to not only change our corner of the world, but also to impact others we may never know.

Sister M. Madeleva Wolff, pray for us!

Reflection Questions

- Sr. M. Madeleva offered her work in all areas as prayer. What are the projects or aspects of your daily life that you could offer as prayer?

- Evangelization is more than just words. It involves meeting people where they are, sometimes speaking to them or simply being quiet, sometimes offering an act of service, or even inviting someone over for dinner. What type of evangelization are you most comfortable with? Why?

- Sr. M. Madeleva was not easily deterred when she encountered obstacles, which helped her pave the way for women to earn advanced degrees in theology. How can you help others by staying true to the path you are on?

Chapter 10:
Anuarite Nengapeta
(Sr. Marie-Clémentine) 1939-1964

Congo

In History

- In the 20th century, European colonialism in Africa reached its peak, with countries like Britain, France, Germany and Belgium all seeking to expand their territories and gain natural resources on the continent. Before the onset of World War I, nearly 90% of the African continent was ruled by a European colonial power.

- Local cultures were often overpowered, and anti-black racism was rife among colonial rulers. Colonial governments were authoritarian, often exploited local rivalries to divide people, and fostered economic dependency. In particular, Belgium's control of the Congo was marred by systemic exploitation of resources, forced labor and violent resistance by many Congolese.

- The end of World War II was a turning point for European colonialism in Africa, with both winners and losers emerging significantly weakened. Further, ideas about universal human rights and the right to self-determination were supported by the newly founded United Nations, encouraging independence movements across the continent. Seventeen African countries declared their independence in 1960 alone.

In Society

- Despite being one of the most violent colonial regimes in Africa, Belgian colonial rule in the Congo took a paternalistic tone. King Leopold II attempted to take on the role of a father providing for his people, rather than providing the opportunity or space for autonomy or input from the native people.

- The country produced crops like cotton, coffee, cacao, oil palms and rubber and also had natural resources including gold, diamonds, copper, tin, cobalt, zinc and uranium.

- Congolese education in the first half of the 1900s was focused primarily on elementary education and was predominantly run by Catholic missions. Higher education was often reserved for society's elite and virtually inaccessible for most of the Congolese people.

Naiyvo nilivyotaka (This is what I wanted).

–Sr. Marie-Clémentine Anuarite Nengapeta

We often think of martyrs as people who lived hundreds or even thousands of years ago, but sadly there are still places today where it is extremely dangerous to be a Christian. It is hard to find a better example of courage in the face of life-threatening danger than Sr. Marie-Clémentine Anuarite Nengapeta. She was a nun and teacher to Congo's poor at a time when Christianity was seen by some as a European influence and a cancer. Her attack and martyrdom at the hands of militant rebels both sobered the attackers and strengthened her sister nuns, who all survived the attacks.

Setting the Stage

Before diving into Blessed Sr. Marie-Clémentine Anuarite Nengapeta's story, let's start with some brief background about the political climate of her time and place, which is an important piece of her story. She was from the country now known as the Democratic Republic of the Congo, a place once controlled by Belgium and known as the Belgian Congo from 1908-1960.

For quite some time in the late 19th and early 20th centuries, large areas of Africa were controlled by European colonial powers such as England, France, and Belgium, among others. Understandably, the colonial powers were not popular among the African people in the areas they'd colonized for many reasons, in some cases including abuses of power. After World War II, the colonial powers began to withdraw; they made varied preparations for the long-term stability of the nations they were leaving, with some colonial powers leaving things in better shape than others.

Belgium's withdrawal from the Congo in 1960 was quite poorly arranged and caused great destabilization and much violence in the area. The area became the Republic of the Congo, and the first prime minister, Patrice Lumumba, was assassinated after less than a year in office. Varying factions vied for control of the country.

The French and Belgian Catholic missions that had been set up during Belgium's colonial rule were identified with the hated European powers and became the targets of violence by a rebel group known as the Simbas. The Simbas particularly hated African Christians, whom they saw as "traitors," and targeted missions staffed by African nuns and priests especially virulently.

Early Life

Against this backdrop, Anuarite Nengapeta was born in Wamba in 1939. At the time, neither of her parents were Christian. The family was part of the Wabudu tribe. She was one of six girls; her father ended up leaving her mother and taking a different wife with the hope of having a son. Her father's departure was hard for her, but she eventually forgave him for leaving the family.

In 1945, she was baptized along with her mother and sisters. At her baptism, she took the name Alphonsine and became Alphonsine Nengapeta before receiving the name Anuarite as the result of a clerical error! Her sister, Leontine Anuarite, took her to register for school. For whatever reason, instead of registering her as Alphonsine Nengapeta, the religious sister at the school registered her under the name Anuarite Nengapeta, and she was known as Anuarite from that day on.

Anuarite greatly admired the nuns in her village and desired to join them, but her mother opposed her desire to pursue a religious vocation. She wanted Anuarite to stay at home and help support the family financially. Anuarite even asked the nuns to admit her to their order, but she was refused due to her youth.

Not to be deterred, Anuarite stowed away on a truck that she knew was taking postulants to the town of Bafwabaka. Her mother interrogated the other village children and learned where Anuarite was a few days later, but she did not force Anuarite to return home.

Anuarite officially became a member of the Congregation of the Holy Family, known as *Jamaa Takatifu*, in 1959. She took the name Sister Marie-Clémentine. Her parents were present at her final vows and even gave the sisters two goats as a sign of support.

Sr. Marie-Clémentine served as a sacristan and cook before becoming an elementary school teacher at Bafwabaka. The sisters lived a peaceful, if somewhat precarious, existence until civil war broke out in earnest in 1964. African Christians quickly became a target, and their diocesan bishop was murdered by the Simbas.

The Fighting Comes to the Sisters

In late 1964, just a few months after the bishop's murder, the Simbas broke into the mission house at Bafwabaka. They told the Mother Superior that they were there to save the sisters from "the Americans." The sisters were packed into a truck and taken away; their destination was Isiro, the Simbas' rebel headquarters.

Along the journey, the Simbas became increasingly drunk and disorderly. They threatened violence and rape but did not carry out their threats that day. They stopped for the night and shoved the sisters into an abandoned mission. The next morning, they pulled them out again and resumed the journey.

The truck was stopped by a car coming in the other direction and carrying one of the Simbas' commanding officers. He caught sight of one of the sisters saying the Rosary and became quite enraged. He demanded that all of the sisters should be stripped of any religious artifacts. All of their rosaries, medals, and so on were taken away from them and roughly scattered into the bush.

Finally, the truck carrying the sisters made it to the Simbas' headquarters in Isiro. The sisters were told that they could all sleep together except for Sr. Marie-Clémentine, who was going to be taken to the officers' quarters for the night because one of the officers, Colonel Ngalo, wanted her (ostensibly) for a wife.

Mother Kasima, the Superior, told Colonel Ngalo that Sr. Marie-Clémentine could not violate her vows by going with him. Mother Kasima and Sr. Marie-Clémentine clung together and refused to let go of each other despite a physical struggle with the officers. Eventually, they were allowed to rejoin the other sisters.

Soon, another drunk officer, Colonel Olombe, came in and tried to force Sr. Marie-Clémentine into his car along with another sister, Sr. Bokuma. He wanted Sr. Bokuma for himself and was trying to force Sr. Marie-Clémentine to succumb to Colonel Ngalo.

When the two sisters refused to go with him, Colonel Olombe became enraged and started beating them with the butt of his revolver. He broke Sr. Bokuma's arm in multiple places and beat Sr. Marie-Clémentine to the ground. Between the savage blows, Sr. Marie-Clémentine told Colonel Olombe that she'd rather be killed than go with him and sacrifice her virginity.

The officer became more enraged. He told the other Simbas nearby that Sr. Marie-Clémentine had attacked him. They stabbed her multiple times with their bayonets before Colonel Olombe shot her in the chest. Before dying just minutes later, Sr. Marie-Clementine managed to utter words of forgiveness to Colonel Olombe with her last breath.

The Simbas were a bit sobered by her death and allowed the other nuns to bring her body into the building where they were imprisoned. Sr. Bokuma was also allowed to return inside, where one of the other sisters tended to her broken arm.

Another Simba, also drunk, later tried to rape some of the other nuns, but they stayed together and warded him off. The situation then calmed down slightly, and the soldiers left the sisters alone, although they did continue to threaten them with rape or death verbally. The government's forces captured Isiro a few days later and released the sisters. Sr. Marie-Clémentine's body was eventually exhumed and reburied, with great ceremony, in Isiro Cathedral.

Her Legacy

In 2009, the Anuarite Woman of Courage in the D.R.C. Prize was established. It is awarded to women in the

Democratic Republic of the Congo who promote democratic values.

Sr. Marie-Clémentine's cause for canonization was opened in 1980 when she was declared venerable. She was beatified in 1985 by Pope John Paul II and is the first member of the Bantu people—an ethnic group in southern Africa comprising various tribes that speak a Bantu language—to be beatified.

During her beatification, Pope John Paul II stressed a few key aspects of Sr. Marie-Clementine's martyrdom. He highlighted her fidelity to her vows even at great personal cost, her intense prayer life that prepared her to sacrifice her life, her commitment to her religious community, and her support of her religious sisters.

Sr. Marie-Clémentine was completely committed to her vocation, even when it meant dying rather than sacrificing her vow. What a beautiful example for all of us, whether our vocation is marriage, religious life, or single life. Sr. Marie-Clémentine cared more about staying true to her promise than to her own life; she truly laid down her life to testify to the sacredness of her vocation.

She also relied heavily on an intense prayer life, and this helped her sustain her strong commitment. Prayer prepares us to face even the most difficult situations and to make the hard choice to follow God regardless of the personal cost. For those of us who are married, we can still follow Sr. Marie-Clémentine's example and rely on a deep prayer life as the foundation of our marriage. For those of us who are single or part of a religious community, a deep prayer life equally solidifies our commitment to that calling.

For Sr. Marie-Clémentine, her commitment wasn't only to her vocation. Her dedication to her community and her community's commitment to each other enabled them to stand together and face down evil as a united group. Sometimes, there is a temptation to throw another person to the wolves, so to speak, to protect our own safety or reputation. Sr. Marie-Clémentine and the Congregation of the Holy Family courageously protected each other and stood up for each other even in the face of great danger.

The sisters supported each other throughout their ordeal and were witnesses to the power of unity in Christ: the spiritual strength that results when a group of people encourages each other to holiness. Sr. Marie-Clémentine's story shows us the power of community and how being part of a strong group of believers can encourage us along our path to holiness.

Her death was also a message that Christianity isn't a political tool; it's a universal truth. She showed that "Christian" does not mean "European"—it means anyone who has given their life to Christ. At a time when being African and Christian was a dangerous identity, she embraced both aspects of who she was and refused to deny either one of them, even when her life was in danger.

The word "martyr" has its roots in a Greek word meaning *witness*, and Sr. Marie-Clémentine was certainly a witness to her faith. She witnessed that staying true to God's promises has a deeper impact than anything the world might bring.

Sr. Marie-Clémentine also teaches us an important lesson about forgiveness. It's easy to hold onto anger and a sense of injustice when we feel that we have been wronged, and especially when we know that we've been unjustly wronged. But Sr. Marie-Clémentine forgave her attackers even as she was dying from their assault. She mirrored God, who forgives over and over when we seek out His mercy, and her example reminds us that we should pursue forgiveness over justice.

Finally, Sr. Marie-Clémentine illustrates the need for determination! She was determined to join the Congregation of the Holy Family, and then she was determined to stay truthful to her vows and keep her body pure. Her determination helped her to focus on the end goal - eternity - instead of the physical danger of the moment. It also empowered her to show both courage *and* mercy. She was determined to resist the Simbas courageously, and she was also determined to forgive her murderer and show the same mercy that God extends to us.

We may not all be called to martyrdom, but we are all called to witness to our faith, as Sr Marie-Clémentine did. Her commitment to her vocation and willingness to put her promises to God above everything else are truly inspiring.

Blessed Sr. Marie-Clémentine Anuarite Nengapeta, pray for us!

Reflection Questions

- Sr. Marie-Clémentine's sisters encouraged her to honor her vows during the attack of the Simbas. How do you encourage those around you to grow in holiness? Do you allow yourself to be positively influenced by those around you?

- Sr. Marie-Clémentine's prayer life prepared her for the day of the Simba attack. What has prayer enabled you to overcome or pursue in your life?

- Sr. Marie-Clémentine modeled forgiveness even at a very young age when her father left her family and again later when she was assaulted. How do you understand forgiveness? Whom or what do you need to forgive?

Chapter 11:
Margarete Sommer 1893-1965

Germany

In History

- After Germany's unconditional surrender on May 7, 1945, at the end of World War II, Germany was divided into four military occupation zones with France, the United Kingdom, the United States and the Soviet Union (U.S.S.R.), each occupying different zones. The city of Berlin was located inside the Soviet-controlled zone, but was similarly divided into east and west zones, with the U.S., U.K., and France controlling the western side and the U.S.S.R. occupying the east.

- In 1949, Germany formally split into two independent nations: the Federal Republic of Germany (FDR or West Germany), allied to the Western democracies, and the German Democratic Republic (GDR or East Germany), allied to the Soviet Union. Berlin was similarly divided into East and West Berlin, with the western side of the city belonging to West Germany.

- Continuing tensions between East and West and a flood of refugees from East to West led to the construction of the Berlin Wall in 1961. This physical barricade dividing the city became one of the most recognized symbols of the Cold War and the struggle between East and West.

In Society

- Following the end of World War II, trials were held in Nuremberg, Germany where prominent Nazi leaders were prosecuted for atrocities, including war crimes, crimes against humanity, and conspiracy to commit further crimes. Nuremberg was chosen because it had been the site of Nazi rallies leading up to the war.

- Antisemitism was still pervasive in Germany after the defeat of the Nazis, with few Jews feeling they could live in the country again. Polls in the second half of the 1940s found that more than 50% of Germans held antisemitic attitudes to some degree. The Jews who remained, only around 15,000, often led secluded lives and interacted primarily with other Jews. An unwillingness by many to face the atrocities of the war also likely contributed to Jewish isolation.

- Few surviving Jews chose to remain in Germany after World War II, and instead, many others decided to emigrate to the United States and Israel, whose nationhood was established in 1948.

The difficulty of this work lies in the fact that those affected are psychologically deeply depressed because of the hopelessness of the efforts (to help them).

–Margarete Sommer

Margarete Sommer was a German Catholic who dedicated her life to serving others, including courageously serving Jewish people during the persecutions of the Nazi regime. Despite a lifetime spent serving others, especially Jewish people both during and after World War II, she was always haunted by the feeling that she should have done more.

Early Life

Margarete was born into a Catholic family in 1893 near Berlin, Germany. During World War I, she served as a nurse in a hospital run by Dominican sisters. She later became a Third Order Dominican.

At the University of Berlin, she studied economics, philosophy, history, and law. She was also a member and, for a short period, the leader of the Catholic student association. Margarete received her doctorate from the University of Berlin in 1924, where she wrote her thesis about prison welfare. There were only about 3,500 female university students in Germany at that time, and it was very unusual for a woman to receive a doctoral degree, yet Margarete persisted in her education.

After completing her PhD, Margarete became a lecturer at the School for Social Welfare of the Pestalozzi-Fröbel House. The School was a training center for social workers. Margarete taught there from 1927 until 1934, when she was forced out for refusing to include Nazi ideology in her lectures. She was under pressure to teach her students that they should force disabled people to be sterilized and was dismissed from her position when she refused to do so.

Margarete, along with her mother and sister, moved to Kleinmachnow on the outskirts of Berlin after she left the School for Social Welfare. She continued working in social welfare and became friends with two priests who later became very well-known for their opposition to antisemitism and vocal stance against the Nazis: Father Bernhard Lichtenberg and Father Franziskus Stratmann.

Nazi Persecution

Father Lichtenberg was interrogated by the Gestapo multiple times before his eventual arrest in 1941, and Father Stratmann was first arrested as early as 1933. Like Margarete, they saw what was happening to the Jewish people and were unafraid to call attention to it despite the personal risk that they faced.

Once the Nazi party came into power, Margarete's work for social welfare was focused on helping the people whom the Nazis classified as "non-Aryans." Starting in 1939, she worked with Father Lichtenberg at the Office of Special Relief of the diocese of Berlin. The Office of Special Relief coordinated aid for Catholic "non-Aryans." After Father Lichtenberg was arrested in 1941, Margarete became the managing director of the Relief Office. Father Lichtenberg later died en route to the concentration camp at Dachau.

As the director of the Office of Special Relief, Margarete had access to deportation lists and helped many people on the lists hide or leave the country. The majority of the people she helped avoid deportation were Christian, but others were Jewish. The Office of Special Relief started out by serving only Jews who had converted to Catholicism, but it quickly moved to serve all Jews regardless of their current religious beliefs.

The Office of Special Relief's original goal was to provide assistance with housing, help finding employment, or support with emigration. But after 1941, its main task was saving Jews in any way possible. Margarete and those she worked with embraced their mission, even at great personal risk. Many of their activities were considered highly criminal under the Nazi laws and would have resulted in a harsh sentence or even death if they had been caught.

At one point, the Office of Special Relief supported approximately 120 Jewish families. Margarete's position as the director was not only administrative. She helped to buy food, pay rent, purchase clothing, engage the services of doctors, and more for Jewish people, as their movements were very restricted by the Nazis.

Outside of her professional work, Margarete also tried to assist the Jewish people by sending aid packages to the Oranienburg-Sachsenhausen concentration camp. She also helped to hide several Jews from the Nazis.

Margarete worked in concert with Father Alfred Brinkmann and his sexton, Robert Kaminski, to hide two men—including a Jewish printer named Erich Wolff—in the crypt at Sacred Heart Church in 1942. She also took in a young girl named Sonja Goldwerth, hiding Sonja in her apartment for a while before taking her to a Catholic asylum for girls. Sonja later said, "For me, she was absolutely a guardian angel," (as cited in Yad Vashem).

Speaking Out Against Nazism

However, Margarete's work was not limited to providing individual aid to those in need. She also stood up against the Nazis in a larger, more public way. Margarete worked with Bishop Konrad Graf von Presying to try to encourage the German bishops to speak out against the Nazis' treatment of the Jewish people and the dangers of Nazi ideology. She also filed reports with Church leaders in Germany about the horrors that the Jews were facing.

She closely monitored the Third Reich's "final solution" and the plans to dissolve "mixed marriages." She sent reports with the information that she'd gathered to the Vatican to try to inform the Vatican about the persecution and deportation of Jews as well as the existence of the concentration camps, such as a report sent in 1942 titled *Report on the Exodus of the Jews.*

The Work Continues Post World War II

After World War II, Margarete continued her relief work. Instead of stepping back and relaxing once the Nazi party had been defeated, she continued to work tirelessly to deal with the aftermath of the Holocaust. She filed death certificates for Jewish Catholics who had been killed, and she helped Jewish people returning to Berlin to rebuild their lives. Post-war Germany was devastated, with insufficient housing and food for its people, and differing opinions on how to help holocaust survivors, or indeed if they deserved any help at all.

During the war, the indiscriminate persecution of Jews created a spirit of solidarity among different religious groups that seemed to evaporate after the fighting had stopped. This was perhaps the most difficult time of Margarete's career and ministry, often having to deal with both societal indifference and depression among the people she was trying to help.

Margarete's home was in the Soviet-controlled zone when Berlin was divided at the end of the war. She helped people escape out of the Soviet zone and into West Berlin until she was finally forced to flee to West Berlin herself in the middle of the night.

Margarete began managing pastoral care for women in the Diocese of Berlin in 1945. In 1949, she became a member of the Community for Christian–Jewish Cooperation. Starting in 1952, she worked in refugee pastoral care. Margarete died in 1965.

Her Legacy

Margarete has been honored—both during her lifetime and posthumously—with several awards and recognitions. She received the Federal Cross of Merit, First Class in 1953 and was included on a list of "Unsung Heroes"—Berliners who stood up to the Nazis and aided "non-Aryans"—in 1961. She also received the designation of "Righteous Among the Nations" from Yad Vashem in 2003.

Despite all of the awards she later received and the huge personal risks that she took during World War II, Margarete never felt that she had done enough to save the Jewish people during the Holocaust. Feelings of guilt haunted her for the rest of her life and spurred her to keep working for others. Her personal involvement with many of the Holocaust survivors meant she knew their stories, struggles, and the impact the war had had on them. She would not rest and point to all the people she had saved; she kept working to help the next person.

Margarete's overwhelming desire to help others reminds us that works of mercy are never done! God doesn't call us to feed one person and check off the list that we've fed the hungry. It's a constant, lifelong call to reach out to others and help them in any way we can. Margarete's example also shows us that sometimes God allows us to struggle as we try to do His work on Earth. Our feelings and consolation may not appear to be His priority, but we can persevere even in the midst of desolation.

According to the Catechism of the Catholic Church, the corporal works of mercy include:

- *feeding the hungry*

- *sheltering the homeless*

- *clothing the naked*

- *visiting the sick and imprisoned*

- *burying the dead*

Margarete's ability to serve others was, in some ways, an extension of her vocation to the single life. As a laywoman, Margarete had the freedom to go where she needed to go and work when she needed to work. As a single woman, she had the freedom to focus her attention where it was needed most. Her state in life helped enable her to assist so many people in so many ways and demonstrates the profound impact and important contributions that can be made by those called to the single life.

Margarete was also unusual in that she was a highly educated, professional woman at a time when education was largely a man's domain, and very few women worked as professionals. But she boldly pursued her studies, never doubting her right to be there, and boldly pursued her career, even when it became politically dangerous for her to do so. Margarete gives us an example of a woman who knew her calling and, without a doubt, stayed true to it regardless of opposition and her own discouragement.

We may not all be called to challenge social norms in pursuing our calling, but it's also almost certain that we will face obstacles at some point, whether large or small. At those times, we can remember Margarete Sommer and her unwavering conviction that as long as she was doing the work God had called her to do, He would open all of the necessary doors for her.

Margarete was also courageous in her willingness to encourage the bishops and other Church leaders to speak out against the Nazis. She had great respect for the Church but also realized that, as humans, the people who make up the Church are not perfect and have their own failings and weaknesses. She wasn't afraid to take the bishops to task—although always through appropriate channels and with respect. For Margarete, the value of human lives was the most important thing, and she was relentless in calling Church leaders to defend people who were being persecuted.

In this way, Margarete gives us another lesson that is still relevant in our time. There may be times when we realize that we need to speak to others about the holiness that God is calling us to live out. Like Margarete, we may need to respectfully, lovingly, and in an appropriate manner, share the teachings of the Gospel.

She certainly practiced what she preached. Margarete's professional career was threatened early on when she refused to bow to the Nazis and subscribe to teaching their policy of forced sterilization. Yet she trusted that God had another plan and was willing to sacrifice her professional position rather than subscribe to something that she knew was morally wrong. We can look at Margarete's example and remember that when we stand up for God, He stands up for us. We may face consequences or backlash for taking a strong stance against things that we know are morally wrong, but we can trust that God is ultimately in control.

It may seem like a fairly ordinary thing to refuse to back down from a belief we know is right, but sometimes that can become an act of extraordinary heroism. It certainly did for Margarete. She took daily action to do things that, in and of themselves, may have seemed inconsequential in other circumstances—buying groceries or clothing for a Jewish family or sending an aid package to a prisoner, for example. However, these things became heroic against the backdrop of Nazi Germany and the risk Margarete knew that she was taking by doing these things, over and over.

Acts of courage don't have to mean facing down an armed enemy or stepping forward to give up your life in someone else's place. Sometimes, acts of courage come in the form of promoting human welfare for all people, of all backgrounds, at all times—just like Margarete Sommer did.

Margarete Sommer, pray for us!

Reflection Questions

- Margarete suffered greatly after World War II when faced with people's indifference about helping the victims of Naziism. Have you ever struggled with the attitudes of others when trying to do works of mercy?

- What people or groups close to you might need some encouragement or help? How can you help them?

- Each woman in this book served God as part of their vocation. As a single woman, it is possible Margarete was better able to serve others than she could have if she was caring for a family. How does your vocation or life stage enable you to be God's hands and feet on Earth?

Chapter 12:

Boleslawa Lament 1862-1946

Poland, Russia

In History

- Nicholas II was the last tzar of Russia, ruling from 1894-1917. He proved an ineffective and autocratic leader who led Russia into a series of costly wars, dismissing those who dared to disagree with him. He and his wife isolated themselves, seeking counsel from the infamous mystic Grigori Rasputin. The general discontent and poor economic conditions led to mass demonstrations and rebellion, and Nicolas's eventual abdication in 1917.

- The Russian Revolution of 1917 included two waves - the first was in February when Tzar Nicholas II was forced to abdicate. The second was in October, when Bolsheviks led by Vladimir Lenin seized power and instituted a Communist government. This sparked a civil war that lasted until 1923 with Lenin's victory and the establishment of the Soviet Union.

- Tzar Nicholas and his family had planned to go to England after his abdication but instead were detained under house arrest in the Ural Mountains in April 1918. Fearing that anti-Bolshevik forces were about to rescue him, in July, the Bolsheviks murdered Nicholas, his wife Alexandra, and their five children in the basement of the house they lived in.

In Society

- The Industrial Revolution reached Russia around the beginning of the 20th century, later than the United States or Western Europe, bringing significant social and political upheaval. Between 1890 and 1910, urbanization and population growth caused the number of people living in major cities like Moscow and St. Petersburg to double, resulting in overcrowding and destitute housing for many.

- Throughout the Russian Revolution, the Bolsheviks attacked religious organizations, which they considered the primary ideological enemy. The economic base of the church was subsequently destroyed, along with programmatic intimidation and persecution of believers, a system that continued during Soviet rule as well.

- In the village of Fatima, Portugal, from May to October 1917, Mary appeared to three Portuguese children to ask them to pray the rosary daily for an end to World War I, for the conversion of sinners and of Russia. She said that if people did not do this, another war would come, more terrible than the first, but that the conversion of Russia would bring peace. Many years later in an interview with Sr. Lucia, one of the children to whom Our Lady of Fatima appeared, she said that the most essential message from Fatima is the importance of fulfilling your daily duty and that praying the rosary can help reinforce your commitment to do this.

We must believe in victory. We shouldn't believe in failures because the works of God can't fail—there's only victory.

–Mother Boleslawa Lament

A woman on a mission, Mother Boleslawa Lament was, in many ways, ahead of her time. She braved the political climate of the early days of Soviet communism to be a resource for Russian Christians, regardless of their denomination. With unwavering trust in God, she focused not on the personal risk she faced, but rather on the things that unite believers, and founded a new order along the way.

Early Life

Boleslawa Lament was born in 1862 in Lowicz, Poland. She had seven younger siblings, although three of them died in childhood. A sensitive child, Boleslawa was greatly affected by her siblings' deaths, even though childhood mortality was much more common during her early years than it is today. She grieved their losses for many years.

Boleslawa's mother was described as a kind-hearted woman, while her father had a reputation for sternness. Boleslawa inherited both of these traits: She was kind, but also serious and somewhat exacting. As a child, she was known to be rather bossy, especially toward her siblings! She attended a school in Lowicz run by Russians, who held very negative attitudes toward Polish Catholics like Boleslawa and her family. She faced much discrimination at school but relied on her faith to help her succeed anyway.

Boleslawa graduated with honors despite the prejudice against her. After finishing school, she earned a certificate as a seamstress and opened a tailor shop with her sister Stanislava.

It wasn't long before Boleslawa heard God calling to her while she was on a religious retreat. In 1884, at age 22, she joined the Congregation of the Family of Mary. She taught in elementary schools and also served the order as a seamstress. The other sisters described her as very prayerful, faithful to her duties, and serious. However, she started to doubt her religious vocation. She wasn't sure whether God was truly calling her to be part of the order, so Boleslawa left the Congregation of the Family of Mary in 1893 before making her final vows.

After leaving the Congregation of the Family of Mary, Boleslawa returned home to her family. However, she remained open to the Lord and began to care for the poor and homeless upon the advice of her spiritual director. Soon afterward, her family moved to Warsaw and again, Boleslawa opened a tailor shop there, this time, with her sister Maria.

Boleslawa's father died in 1894 during a cholera epidemic, and she quickly took over the financial responsibility of providing for the rest of the family. In addition to running the tailor shop with Maria to support her family, Boleslawa also became the director of a local homeless shelter. She visited the poor and the sick and was especially devoted to making sure that the people she visited and those who took refuge in the shelter had access to the sacraments.

Boleslawa continued to reflect on her vocation and whether God was calling her to religious life. She became a member of the Third Order Franciscans and became friends with a Capuchin friar, Father Honorat Kozminski, who worked with the underground Church in Russia and Poland.

Her younger brother Stefano, who was in seminary and studying to become a priest, tragically died in 1900. After his death, Boleslawa deeply felt a renewed call to religious life. She turned to Father Kozminski for counsel, who suggested that Boleslawa travel to Russia and work with the underground Church there to help strengthen people's faith despite the persecution they faced.

Working in Russia

Boleslawa moved to Mogilev, Russia, and met a woman named Leocadia Gorczynska, who ran a weaving school. Boleslawa quickly realized that this was a valuable skill that she could pass on to young girls to give them a trade and a way to earn a living, so she studied weaving with Leocadia.

Soon after moving to Russia, Boleslawa combined her administrative skills—which she'd learned from managing the tailor shop and overseeing the homeless shelter—with the call she'd been hearing from God. She started her own religious order: the Congregation of the Missionary Sisters of the Holy Family. The order was officially founded in 1905 in Mogilev, with Boleslawa and a few other women (including Leocadia Gorczynska) as the first sisters. Father Felice Wiercinski was their spiritual director.

The order's goal was to promote Christian unity, particularly between the Catholic and Orthodox churches, along with serving the poor and teaching young girls about what it meant to live as a Christian.

Boleslawa was the first superior, becoming "Mother Boleslawa."

The sisters' ministry grew rapidly; they moved to St. Petersburg, Russia in 1907 and helped educate young people there. Mother Boleslawa also worked to form relationships between Catholic and Orthodox Christians, hoping that they could help each other remain faithful despite political persecution. She knew that they would be more successful in facing persecution if the churches were united and working in harmony. In 1913, the order expanded into Finland, where the sisters ran a boarding school for teenage girls.

Russian Christians were facing more persecution starting in 1917 than they had under the czars for the previous few decades—due to both World War I and the Bolshevik revolution. The sisters persisted in their work for a few years, but Mother Boleslawa and the rest of her order had to flee Russia in 1921 because it had become too dangerous for them to remain there. They returned to Poland and opened a new house in the eastern part of the country.

Rebuilding in Poland

Leaving Russia was a great spiritual and financial loss for Mother Boleslawa and the Congregation. Fleeing Russia meant that they had to abandon many of their plans to share Christianity with the people they served, and it also caused great material losses that left the order in deep poverty. But Mother Boleslawa saw God's hand in everything that happened, despite the challenges, and continued putting His will first. She trusted that if He took them out of Russia in abject poverty, He would provide a way for them to continue.

The Congregation began growing again after relocating to Poland. Mother Boleslawa eventually stepped down as the Mother General of the order in 1935. At the time of her "retirement," the Congregation had 33 houses. Its members numbered over 170 sisters, with 35 more women either in the novitiate or postulant stage of discerning their vocation.

After stepping away from her leadership role in the Congregation, Mother Boleslawa moved to Bialystok. She opened schools and educated children, continuing on with her work despite increasingly poor health. During World War II, the Congregation's work changed. They started ministering to the needs of people who had been affected by the war, especially homeless children. The Congregation was, once again, affected materially by war as the ravages of World War II destroyed much of Europe.

Mother Boleslawa became paralyzed in 1941. Even though she was bedridden and suffering greatly, she continued to advise the other sisters. She also prayed for them fervently until her death in 1946. She was buried at the Congregation's convent in Ratowo, in eastern Poland. Mother Boleslawa used the final years of her life to prepare herself to return to God. She had always wanted to spread God's glory and had offered herself to the Sacred Heart of Jesus, which was a source of great strength and comfort to her in later years.

Her Legacy

Mother Boleslawa was named a Servant of God in 1975 and beatified by Pope John Paul II in 1991 during his apostolic trip to Poland. Her friend Father Kozminski, who had encouraged her to help the Church in Russia, has also been beatified. This is a testimony to the importance of having good and holy friends who will encourage us toward heaven! The Congregation of the Missionary Sisters of the Holy Family is still active today. The order has houses in Europe, Africa, and the U.S.

Even though the Congregation lost almost everything twice—first in the Russian Revolution and then during the devastation of World War II—Mother Boleslawa did not despair and she encouraged her sisters to have faith. She kept persevering, thanks to the strength that she derived from prayer. She reminds us that prayer is what sustains us and allows us to withstand material hardships because prayer unites us to God.

Mother Boleslawa's deep prayer life helped her discern her calling to the religious life and balance that with the need to help her family. She was not proud and did not desire to put herself first, but instead, she gave all glory to God.

Perhaps, the clearest example of her humility was her decision to step down as the Congregation's superior in 1935. She realized that her health was becoming poor and that she could no longer minister to the needs of the community as effectively as she once had. Instead of allowing her pride to insist that she remain the leader of the order she had founded, Mother Boleslawa put the order's needs above hers. She did what was best for the order—even though it meant putting herself in the background—and ceded her position to another sister so that God's work could continue on without any obstruction.

Promoting Christian Unity

Mother Boleslawa's commitment to ecumenism is also inspiring. She particularly worked to bring together

Catholic and Orthodox believers, knowing that Christians are stronger when they are united than when they are separated. Mother Boleslawa believed that the Christians worshiping in secret in Russia had more in common than not. Importantly, she was calling for Christian unity and dialogue decades before Vatican II focused on ecumenism. She understood the importance of Christians coming together to talk and find points of unity long before it became a movement in the wider Church.

Mother Boleslawa's life also shows us that understanding the time that you live in is necessary for understanding how to fulfill the call that God has given to you. She saw the need for Catholic Christians and Orthodox Christians to rise above their differences and work together to spread the Gospels despite the persecution they faced, and she answered that call without fear. In addition, rather than assigning one particular type of service to the Congregation, she founded the Congregation with a general goal of serving and then matched the type of service they offered to the particular need of the community at that moment in time—whether that was education, food, shelter, or evangelization.

Now, we live in a different time, and God's call to us might look different. Most of us probably aren't called to start a religious order in the Russian underground church, but we might be called to participate in a prayer ministry, mentor someone during their journey to Christianity, or guide our children to grow in faith. The important thing is for us to answer that call with boldness and fearlessness!

Like Mother Boleslawa, we can trust that if God is calling us to a task, then He will equip us with whatever we need to accomplish it. Mother Boleslawa didn't let material poverty or the threat of physical violence stop her from responding to God's call, and neither should we. She trusted that He would provide, and He always did. Her story is a reminder to us that we can confidently trust in His providence.

Mother Boleslawa was fearless in her reliance on God, and she was also fearless in her willingness to follow Him wherever He was calling her. The threat of Russian persecution and the ravages of World War II did not discourage her from going out and serving people. We are also called to fearlessness! She did not hesitate to put herself in physical danger when she knew that she was spiritually following the Lord. Like Mother Boleslawa, we can put our spiritual growth above our physical desires. After all, our ultimate goal is eternity—and that depends much more on spiritual courage than on physical comfort.

Mother Boleslawa was prudent as well. She understood when it was time to relocate in order for the Congregation's good work to continue. As difficult as it might have been to give up all of their houses in Russia, she wasn't afraid to set a new course once it became clear to her that remaining in Russia was no longer judicious. She balanced prudence and courage. Through the intercession of the Holy Spirit, God willing, we can do the same.

Her devotion to the Sacred Heart of Jesus also sustained her faith, particularly during difficult times. Like Mother Boleslawa, we can take refuge in the Sacred Heart of Jesus. Even ordinary actions can become extraordinary gifts when they are offered to His most Sacred Heart.

Blessed Boleslawa Lament, pray for us!

Reflection Questions

- Have people or groups with religious beliefs different from yours enriched your faith? If so, how?

- As a young woman, Boleslawa struggled to discern if God was calling her to religious life or not. Have you struggled to understand where and how God was calling you to serve?

- If faced with a choice of living through religious persecution or financial devastation like Mother Boleslawa was, what would you choose? Why?

Chapter 13:
Daphrose Rugamba 1944-1994
Rwanda
In History

- Rwanda began the 20th century as a German colony. However, the German defeat in World War I meant that in 1919, Rwanda was placed under the administration of the League of Nations and was later passed to Belgium. In 1935, Belgium established a national identification scheme based on ethnicity and initially favored the Rwandan king and ruling elite, all from the Batutsi clan.

- Over time, the Batutsi's political party, the Union Nationale Rwandaise (UNAR), began calling for Rwandan independence. Belgian authorities shifted support to another party, PARMEHUTU, which was founded on sectarian ethnic ideas. In 1959, ethnic violence began with PARMEHUTU sanctioning violence against the Batutis.

- This tension sparked an organized effort to overthrow the monarchy. Elections in 1960 gave overwhelming support to the Hutus at the local level, and a coup in January 1961 brought an all-Hutu government to power. Belgium granted Rwandan independence on July 1, 1962.

In Society

- Ethnic tensions and violence in the late 1950s and early 1960s caused a diaspora of Tutsis into other countries. By the mid-1960s, more than half of the Tutsi population lived outside Rwanda.

- Armed conflict between ethnic groups continued throughout the rest of the 20th century, as Rwandan refugees sought to return to the country and regain their previous standing. In 1988 the Rwandan Patriotic Front (RPF) was founded in Uganda, primarily of Tutsi exiles. In 1990, the RPF launched an attack on Rwanda with a force of 7,000 fighters and all Tutsis in the country were labeled as accomplices.

- In April 1994, the military government launched a campaign to eliminate both the Tutsi minority and moderate Hutus by publishing target lists and leveraging hate radio widely. More than 1 million people were killed in only four months at the hands of the military, armed militias and even trained civilians. In July the armed branch of the RPF was able to oust the military government and take control of the country.

To be on Jesus's lap, or on his chest, to be with him simply, even without saying anything, even in sleep, that is adoration!

–Daphrose Rugamba

Imagine the most committed person you know. Someone who does what they say they will, no matter what. Now multiply that by 100, and you might come close to imagining someone like Daphrose Rugamba. A faithful wife and mother of ten, Daphrose prayed for her husband's conversion for 17 difficult years before they finally found happiness, only a few years before ethic violence and civil war would ravage their native Rwanda and their lives.

Faith-Filled Beginnings

In 1944, in Cyanika, Rwanda, Daphrose Mukasanga was born into a large Catholic family. The family was loving and pious, and her parents nurtured Daphrose in her Catholic faith. As a child, she wanted to be a nun after attending school in a nearby convent. However, God had other plans and she eventually became a teacher.

In 1965, Daphrose married Cyprien Rugamba. Their relationship was initially one of obligation rather than passion. Cyprien had been engaged to Daphrose's cousin, Xaverina Mukahigiro, but tragically, Xaverina was murdered in 1963 in an ethnicity-related massacre. Under Rwandan custom, Cyprien fulfilled their engagement and his commitment to the family by asking to marry Daphrose.

Cyprien and Daphrose's Life Together

They didn't marry right away. Instead, they took some time to date and even ended up falling in love before their wedding in 1965. But the honeymoon phase didn't last long. Daphrose was still a staunch Catholic. Cyprien had attended seminary in the 1950s when he was in his 20s, but later discovered the writings of anti-Catholic existential philosophers and fell away from his faith. In fact, he ended up rejecting the Church completely and became a stringent atheist. He made fun of Daphrose for her faith and her intense prayer life—even going so far as to break her crucifixes.

Professionally, Cyprien was a renowned artist. He was a singer, composer, and choreographer who founded the Rwandan National Ballet. Several of his songs are still well-known in Rwanda even today. Cyprien's work embraced traditional Rwandan styles, which were fast falling out of favor during that time. He also worked as an administrator for the Rwandan government and created a cultural center to encourage others to create traditional Rwandan art so that it didn't totally disappear. Cyprien had a reputation as a champion of the arts, and he achieved a certain level of national prestige as a result.

Cyprien's professional achievements brought the couple a certain level of material comfort. However, despite their material comfort, they faced many challenges in their marriage in addition to the divide in their beliefs. Their first child died during Daphrose's labor. After that, someone spread false rumors about Daphrose that Cyprien heard and, sadly, believed.

He packed up her things and "returned" Daphrose to her family, which was highly insulting in Rwandan culture. They remained separated for several months until

Cyprien eventually asked for Daphrose's forgiveness and took her back into their home. Throughout this ordeal, she had never stopped praying for Cyprien and their reconciliation.

Although they were back together, Cyprien was unfaithful to their marriage vows and even fathered an illegitimate child, in addition to the couple's own nine children. But Daphrose persisted in her faith. She refused to criticize Cyprien to her friends and prayed for him fervently. Her strong belief in the sanctity of marriage never wavered, despite Cyprien's actions.

In fact, Daphrose's faith was so strong that she even went so far as to adopt Cyprien's illegitimate daughter into their family. She took all 10 children to Mass regularly, with his consent.

After 17 years of a troubled marital relationship, Cyprien became quite ill. The mysterious illness affected all of his senses including his sight and hearing—something that was quite a blow for a well-known artist. But Daphrose cared for him tenderly. It was as if all of the years of infidelity and ill-treatment had never happened. Her example started to change Cyprien's heart and made him wonder about her strong faith.

They eventually set off for Europe to seek treatment for Cyprien's illness. On their way, he began to write a song about death, with what he saw as his impending death on his mind. As he began to write, the love of Jesus filled Cyprien's heart. He was completely transformed and had a radical conversion back to Catholicism.

But that wasn't all that he experienced. In addition to his conversion, Cyprien was miraculously cured of his illness. He saw his cure as the fruit of all Daphrose's long years of prayer.

New Beginnings

After this profound experience, their marriage was totally transformed. Cyprien asked forgiveness for his years of infidelity and ill-treatment. Daphrose forgave him and the couple began to serve others joyfully. They welcomed everyone and built their home into a true domestic church.

The family was committed to prayer and charity, and they had a particular compassion for street orphans. Cyprien began composing songs that praised God. Daphrose and Cyprien went on a pilgrimage to France in 1989. During their pilgrimage, they discovered the Emmanuel Community. They identified so strongly with the community's charisms that 1990 the two of them founded the Emmanuel Community in Rwanda.

The Emmanuel Community meets in small groups, known as *households*, to serve God through evangelization and prayer. The community's special charisms are adoration, compassion, and evangelization. Cyprien saw the Emmanuel Community as a place of unity irrespective of one's ethnic group, and they dedicated themselves to growing the community. As a result of their labor, it grew at a rapid pace despite increasing political tensions in Rwanda.

The couple started a ministry in 1992 devoted to helping orphaned children roaming the streets. The ministry was known as the *Centre Cyprien et Daphrose Rugamba* (CECYDAR). Through their ministry, Daphrose and Cyprien bathed and fed orphans before sharing the

Gospel with them, teaching them about Jesus, and witnessing God's love.

Growing Ethnic Hostility in Rwanda

During the early 1990s, tensions between the Hutu and Tutsi tribes continued to build. The Hutus were the ethnic majority in Rwanda, and there was strong animosity between the Hutus and the Tutsis, an ethnic minority. Cyprien and Daphrose were both ethnically Hutu, but they stood up for the Tutsis and affirmed their dignity as human beings. They saw the Emmanuel Community as a place where Hutus and Tutsis could come together and their differences wouldn't matter because, as Cyprien said, "We only have one party—that of Jesus" (as cited in *Cyprien and Daphrose Rugamba*, n.d.).

In addition to working for unity through the Emmanuel Community, Cyprien also used his position as a well-known artist to take a stance. He publicly called for the ethnicity listing to be removed from people's identity cards. Cyprien and Daphrose knew their stance on unity between the Hutus and Tutsis put them and their family in danger, but rather than fleeing the country, they chose to stay in Rwanda and put their trust in God.

The situation in Rwanda came to a head in the spring of 1994 when many Hutus rose up and massacred Tutsis along with the Hutus who publicly supported them. Because of their support for Tutsis and their work toward unity, the Rugamba family was high on the list of people targeted during the genocide.

Cyprien and Daphrose were murdered on April 7, 1994, in the early days of the genocide along with six of their children: Ermerita, Serge, Cyrdy, Dacy, Cyrdina, and Ginie. The family had spent the previous night in adoration at their home; they had received special permission to have the Blessed Sacrament present in the tabernacle of their home chapel. The assassins gunned down the family and then fired into the tabernacle. When the Rugambas' bodies were discovered, they were covered with hosts.

Their Legacy
Cyprien and Daphrose were declared "heroic in virtue" and named Servants of God in 2015. Their cause for canonization is open. Their ministry, CECYDAR, is still in operation. It takes in roughly 100 children at a time and provides them with academic, spiritual, and vocational formation.

In addition to CECYDAR, the Rugambas' legacy lives on in many other ways. Their marriage is a shining example of God's ability to heal and repair even the most fractured relationships. Daphrose spent 17 years praying for Cyprien, and after 17 years of strain and discord, their marriage was restored and became joyful, strong, and Christ-centered.

Daphrose trusted, for those 17 long years, that the Lord heard her prayer and would answer in His time. And her faith was rewarded abundantly! Many of us are familiar with St. Monica and the way that her years of prayer for her son St. Augustine were answered. Now, through the witness of Daphrose and Cyprien Rugamba, we have another beautiful example of the power of faithful prayer and God's ability to transform a hardened heart.

The Power of Prayer
Even though Cyprien's conversion came about through extraordinary means, Daphrose's part in it is not out of

reach for most of us. She prayed for him without fail and trusted God to do the rest. Prayer plus trust equaled space for God to do His work and effect something amazing. That's definitely a method that is accessible to anyone, no matter what situation they are seeking to resolve. Pray frequently, trust completely, and leave it up to God to do the rest!

This also shows us that faithfulness is rewarded. While praying for someone's conversion once or twice is simple, it takes true faithfulness to continue that prayer for 17 years. It would have been easy and understandable for Daphrose to give up and stop believing that God would change Cyprien's heart as the years went by and he remained an atheist. But she never stopped trusting in God; she never stopped praying, and those prayers were eventually rewarded in abundance. Cyprien didn't just return to the Catholic Church out of a sense of obligation; he returned completely on fire for the Lord and in love with his faith.

Daphrose demonstrated another quality throughout their marriage: respect for Cyprien as head of their home, even when he wasn't acting like a very good leader. She continued to respect his position in the family regardless of his behavior. The respect that she showed, whether or not he deserved it, eventually opened his eyes and contributed to his conversion.

Once Cyprien joined Daphrose in leading his family toward Christ, their home became a place of harmony and joy! The Rugamba family welcomed everyone and saw them all as having equal dignity as children of God. Ethnicity and economic standing didn't matter to them. They lived in harmony with those around them. That sense of harmony had its roots in their family life.

Daphrose served her children as the foundation of their ministry to others. She made to sure take care of their domestic church first and to share her love for the Lord with her children. Her ministry was first to her family and second to the community around her.

Daphrose and Cyprien's participation in the community is another key element of their story. From the beginning of time, it's been clear that we are all made to live in community. We function best when we're supported by others. Daphrose and Cyprien, with their work to establish the Emmanuel Community, lived out that call to community. They created a place where people could come together to encourage each other to draw closer to the Lord.

Strong community doesn't arise by accident; Daphrose, along with Cyprien, put in the work to create it. Their leadership and their example helped the community to grow and prosper. In fact, the Emmanuel Community in Rwanda is one of the largest Emmanuel Communities in the world today.

For Daphrose and Cyprien, community didn't just include the people who looked like them, talked like them, lived like them, and thought like them. They expanded their community to include people from different ethnic and socioeconomic backgrounds. The couple heroically worked to bring people together, even when doing so meant the threat of physical violence.

Their community also included the children living on the streets. Those children weren't invisible to Daphrose and Cyprien. They were children of God and thus worthy of love and attention. The Rugambas remind us to open our arms to the marginalized people in our society and welcome them into our community and our Church.

Daphrose might not immediately strike us as the boldest of women; she was quite traditional in her role as a wife and mother, and she worked hand in hand with her husband to lead their ministries. But her boldness shines out in more subtle ways. She was bold with her prayer when she asked, for 17 years, that Cyprien would be converted. She was bold in her faith when she trusted God and stayed in Rwanda despite the political turmoil. And above all, she was bold in love: love for her husband, her family, her community, and her Church.

Servant of God Daphrose Rugamba, pray for us!

Reflection Questions

- Have you witnessed or experienced a conversion of the heart, like Cyprien had? What is your experience with the power of prayer?

- Daphrose's 17 years of prayer for Cyprien's conversion were an amazing testament to her tenacity. She also had regular practices in her spiritual life, like attending daily Mass. What daily habits can you develop to remain persistent in prayer without becoming discouraged if God's timeline is longer than yours?

- Daphrose had great trust in God's providence to honor her marriage vows when Cyprien was unfaithful and insulting to her. Do you trust in His providence to resolve difficult situations in your life, or do you attempt to resolve them on your own

Chapter 14:
Maria Rita de Souza Brito Lopes Pontes (Sr. Irmã Dulce Lopes Pontes) 1914-1992
Brazil

In History

- The political landscape varied greatly in 20th century Brazil. Brazil started the 1900s as a republic dominated by large coffee producers in which only wealthy landowners could vote. The societal conflict this generated eventually led to a military dictatorship from 1964 to 1989. The 1989 elections brought a democratically elected government to power, beginning a new period for Brazilian politics.

- The 20th century was also a time of significant economic change and growth, beginning as an agrarian, largely rural, country and developing into an urban, industrial society. The second half of the century saw both diversification and modernization of agriculture and other industries, so that by the end of the 1900s Brazil had a strong services and finance sector, in addition to being one of the most important grain producers in the world.

- Brazil is the fifth largest country in the world and enjoys abundant resources, such as significant mineral reserves and arable land for agriculture. While this has been developed more in the southern regions of the country, improved transportation is making it possible to access these resources.

In Society

- In the early 20th century, most Brazilians lived in rural areas, but with increased industrialization, more and more people moved to large cities. The migration was largely from north to south, especially to the state of São Paulo, which became the wealthiest and most populated state in Brazil. By the end of the 20th century, four-fifths of the population lived in an urban area.

- Such widespread and rapid urbanization created several challenges, including an unprecedented demand for housing. This made urban land prices skyrocket so that many middle-class people had to live in very small apartments and poor people in shanty towns called *favelas*.

- The early 1900s brought a literary renaissance to the country with authors writing about their daily experiences. One prime example comes from Euclides da Cunha's historical story, *Os Sertões*, (Rebellion in the Backlands), about the conflict between government forces and a band of separatists in the interior state of Bahia, a largely untamed place. In the narrative, Cunha reflects on the "two Brazils" and the divide between rural and urban ways of life.

If there were more love, the world would be different; if we loved more, there would be less war. It all comes down to this: Do your best for your brother, and therefore there will be peace on earth.

–Sr. Irmã Dulce Lopes Pontes

Sr. Irmã Dulce Lopes Pontes was a Brazilian nun who founded one of the largest and most respected charitable organizations in Brazil. She was nominated twice for the Nobel Peace Prize for her work with the poor in Bahia, which famously started in her convent's chicken yard in 1949. Now thousands of people come to this very same location to receive free medical treatment every day.

Beginnings of a Life of Charity

Maria Rita de Souza Brito Lopes Pontes was born in Salvador de Bahia, Brazil in 1914. Her father was a dentist and professor who was also dedicated to providing charity for the poor. Her mother, Dulce, died when Maria was only six, and her aunts helped to raise her. She was a free-spirited child who loved to play soccer and fly kites.

Maria had a life-changing experience at the tender age of 13. One of her aunts took her to visit a slum neighborhood—called a *favela* in Brazil. The intense poverty she saw in the favela profoundly moved Maria. She began inviting the poor and the sick into her home to care for them. She gave them haircuts and tended to their wounds. Maria also developed a strong devotion to Saint Thérèse of Lisieux and imitated Saint Thérèse 's message of doing small acts with great love.

Maria felt a call to religious life as a young girl, but her father encouraged her to become a teacher. She graduated from high school with a teaching qualification. However, by this time, her father had relented, and with her father's blessing, Maria joined the Missionary Sisters of the Immaculate Conception of the Mother of God. She took the name Dulce to honor her mother and became Sr. Irmã Dulce Lopes Pontes, although she was more commonly known as Sr. Dulce.

Religious Life

After joining the order, Sr. Dulce returned to her hometown of Salvador de Bahia and began teaching. However, her deep love for the poor persisted, and she always found time to serve them. She helped found the Sao Francisco's Workers' Union—which was the first Christian worker movement in Bahia—and opened a school for the union workers' children.

In addition to teaching, she continued to tend to the poor that she encountered. As her reputation grew, more and more people sought out Sr. Dulce to ask for help. She started housing the homeless and sick people who came to her in abandoned buildings that were located in a part of Bahia known as "Rat Island." She brought food and medical care to the people housed in the abandoned buildings. But it wasn't long before Sr. Dulce's "patients" were evicted.

Next, she tried moving the homeless people who she was caring for to an abandoned fish market, but they were evicted again. So, in 1949, Sr. Dulce received permission from her Mother Superior to house her homeless patients in the convent's henhouse. The only stipulation was that she had to take care of the chickens, too. Well, Sr. Dulce's solution to caring for the chickens was quite practical: she fed them to her patients! She made sure that the people she was caring for had not just a place to stay but a full belly, as well!

The Start of the Charitable Works Foundation

Her ministry of caring for the poor and the sick continued to expand. In 1959, Sr. Dulce founded her own charitable organization: the Charitable Works Foundation of Sister Dulce (*Obras Sociais Irmã Dulce*), also known as OSID. The organization helped the poor in a variety of ways, whether that was through meals, medical care, or meeting a different need. OSID is still active today; it is now one of the largest charitable healthcare organizations in Brazil. It serves over 3.5 million people each year.

Sr. Dulce tried to greet every person who came through OSID's soup line herself. She truly looked at them to see the person in front of her; then, she listened to what they needed, and she tried to meet it. No need was too small or insignificant for her to address. OSID offered services like haircuts and transportation to the people who came looking for help, in addition to serving meals and providing access to medical care. Sr. Dulce was even known to pick people up and carry them to the hospital herself if there was no other way to get them there.

Her willingness to physically transport people to the hospital herself is even more impressive because Sr. Dulce suffered from lung problems for the last 30 years of her life. Her health problems were so severe that 70% of her lung capacity was compromised, and she spent over 16 months in the hospital near the end of her life due to her respiratory impairments. But she never let her own physical infirmity deter her from working to help the poor, the sick, and the disabled.

Sr. Dulce came to be known as the "Brazilian Mother Teresa" and the "Good Angel of Bahia." She was nominated for the Nobel Peace Prize in 1988. Near the end of her life, in 1990, Pope John Paul II visited her in the hospital during a trip to Brazil. The original location of her efforts, the congregation's old henhouse, is now the Santo Antonio Hospital, which specializes in cancer treatment and still serves those in poverty.

Sr. Dulce died in 1992 and was initially buried at the Basilica of Our Lady of the Immaculate Conception in Bahia. She was beatified in 2011 and canonized in 2019—the third-fastest cause for canonization in history. During the beatification process, she was exhumed in 2010, and her body was found to be incorrupt. She was later reburied at the Santo Antônio Chapel.

A Bias Towards Action

One of the beautiful aspects of Sr. Dulce's life is her focus on the individual, not the institutional. She saw the people in front of her and cared for them as individuals. She didn't wait around to send them through an institutional, one-size-fits-all process. Instead, she listened to their unique needs and figured out a way to meet them. She didn't worry about putting formal processes and procedures in place first.

Sr. Dulce didn't wait to set up a charitable foundation and fundraise to buy a building; she picked people up out of the streets and put them in abandoned buildings that were conveniently located nearby. She didn't wait until she was able to relocate the chickens and build a brand-new structure; she fed the chickens to the poor and then moved them into the now-vacant henhouse. Sr. Dulce was a woman of action.

This isn't to say that she saw institutions, particularly charitable ones, as unimportant. After all, she eventually formed her own charitable institution! Sr. Dulce cared for the individual first and then let the formal institution grow out of that as a secondary fruit. Serving the individual planted the seed for the institution to be formed, and not vice versa.

All too often, it's easy for us to hide behind an institution (or the lack of one) as an excuse. We either wait for the organization to tell us how to serve others, or we feel like we can't serve others because there isn't a formal process in place. But maybe, we just need to be a little more like Sr. Dulce, who looked at the person first and figured out the organization later.

It is especially incredible to consider all the acts of service Sr. Dulce accomplished in spite of her own health challenges! She could easily have pointed to her impaired lung capacity as a reason for staying in her convent and taking up a more contemplative approach to life. Instead, she went out into the streets and literally carried people to the hospital.

Sr. Dulce clearly had an immense trust in God. She trusted that He would allow her to keep working despite her physical frailties. She also trusted that He would provide for whatever she needed, such as shelter for the homeless people she cared for. Sr. Dulce identified the need, turned it over to God in prayer, and trusted in Him to do the rest.

Sr. Dulce knew the power of prayer and she let her prayer spur her into action. In a sense, her prayers were the seed, and her actions were the fruit that grew as a result.

With her focus on taking action, Sr. Dulce refused to be overwhelmed by the immense need that she faced. She realized that doing *something*, no matter how small, was better than doing nothing. As a 13-year-old, she knew that she wouldn't be able to alleviate all of the poverty in the favela, but she also knew that she could give a few haircuts to restore dignity and a sense of self-worth to some of the people living there. So, she did just that.

She was present with the person in front of her, and she did whatever small things she could to help meet his or her needs. Gradually, Sr. Dulce's efforts began to snowball until she was able to meet the needs of more and more people, either through her own actions or through the people inspired by her actions.

The Importance of Every Act of Service

Sr. Dulce didn't put her focus on extraordinary acts of courage and daring. Instead, she was guided by the example of St. Thérèse of Lisieux to emphasize small acts of love. She butchered some chickens and made soup to feed the hungry, she gave someone a haircut, or she provided a ride to the bus stop. These are things that anyone can do. It was the love and the care that Sr. Dulce put into such simple actions that made them so profound. She truly *saw* the person she was serving, and she looked at them with the eyes of Christ.

Her story also shows us the profound inspiration that can result from taking another saint as a role model. Sr. Dulce looked to St. Thérèse of Lisieux and was guided by her life; in turn, maybe a future saint is out there and ready to be guided by the life of Sr. Dulce. Regardless of the differences in country, language, or century, we can always find something to imitate when we learn about the saints' lives and the type of heroic virtue that they demonstrate. St. Thérèse of Lisieux encourages us to look at the people around us with great love, and that's what Sr. Dulce did.

Sr. Dulce didn't look at people and see their differences. Rather, when she looked at people she saw Christ, and she loved them. She encouraged everyone to do the best they could for the people around them and saw this as the way to solve the world's larger problems. Sr. Dulce knew the importance of needing to "act local" long before it became a popular marketing slogan.

Maybe we don't live near a favela, but all of us can serve someone nearby and look at them with the eyes of Christ in the process. Perhaps we can bring a meal to someone who's just had surgery or a new baby, watch a friend's children for a few hours so that they can go to an appointment, or sit with an older neighbor and listen to them talk. Sr. Dulce's example reminds us that when we serve others, we bring them Christ, and we also serve Christ present in them.

Saint Irmã Dulce Lopes Pontes, pray for us!

Reflection Questions

- Sr. Dulce first felt drawn to serve the poor in an experience she had as a 13-year-old. How have your childhood experiences shaped your life? Your spirituality? Your service?

- Are you more drawn to a life of active service, like Sr. Dulce, or a life of contemplation, like Sr. Teresa Benedicta?

- Do you have a "saintly mentor," like St. Thérèse of Lisieux was for Sr. Dulce?

Chapter 15:
Maria Quattrocchi 1884-1965

Italy

In History

- The Italian Economic Miracle refers to the period of time after World War II until the mid-1960s and is marked by significant economic and industrial gains in the country. U.S. aid in the form of the Marshall Plan, coupled with light-touch regulation and taxation, created a foundation to rebuild and expand Italian infrastructure and industry.

- The economic boom was especially strong in northern areas like Lombardy and Piedmont. A northern industrial triangle emerged, with production of goods such as automobiles, clothing, electronics, and other items. This also created wide-spread migration from southern regions to the more industrial north.

- Southern Italy did not develop at the same rate as the north, with the average income per person in the south coming in at half that of the north in 1950. Policies attempting land reform and industrial development were not as successful there.

In Society

- In less than 20 years following the end of World War II, Italy was transformed from a largely agrarian society to an industrial, urban country.

With an increase in the average Italian's income, ownership of goods like household appliances and cars also grew.

- Italian mass media was dominated by the *Radiotelevisione Italiana* (RAI), which began broadcasting on the radio in the 1920s and added television in the 1950s. Advertising on these platforms influenced consumerism in society.

- The post-war years also saw Italians grappling with the cultural effects of fascism, and the desire to redefine the national identity was strong. Some called for a "new culture," while others saw fascism as an interruption to the established Italian way of life. Others leaned towards neorealism, which focused on the grittiness of daily life.

The family has to be a sanctuary where God is always glorified.

–Maria Quattrocchi

Could doing the laundry be on your road to heaven? Or getting up at night with a sick child? A wife, a mother and a professional, Maria Quattrocchi is a beautiful example of how an ordinary domestic life can become a path to holiness.

A Noble Start

She was born Maria Corsini in 1884 in Italy to a noble family who was cultured and valued education. Maria was very well educated and eventually received a degree from La Sapienza, a top university in Rome, and after graduation she became a university professor. Maria enjoyed music and she volunteered with both Catholic and secular institutions. She was active in Women's Catholic Action and served as a Red Cross nurse in Ethiopia.

The Corsini family was friends with another family, the Beltrames. Their son Luigi had been "adopted" by his uncle, who was childless, and he eventually took his uncle's last name, Quattrocchi, to honor that relationship. Maria and Luigi (Beltrame) Quattrocchi became friendly. When Luigi briefly fell ill, Maria sent him a picture of the Madonna of Pompeii and an encouraging letter. After that, their relationship intensified, and they were married in Rome about a year later, in 1905.

Luigi was also well-educated; he'd completed a law degree at La Sapienza. He eventually went on to become an honorary deputy attorney general of Italy and rub shoulders with the political leaders who helped to rebuild Italy after the horrors of World War II and fascism. But despite his professional success, the Quattrocchi family remained humble and grounded in God.

Luigi wasn't always on fire for his faith. In fact, he was a lukewarm Catholic, at best, when he and Maria married. But she was a pious, holy woman who gradually influenced Luigi's faith.

The couple had four children in total: Filippo, Stefania, Cesare, and Enrichetta. The first three children were born in their first four years of marriage, and Maria was very sick with all her pregnancies, and she despaired with each one. During her second pregnancy, she even wrote to her husband, "Who will give me the strength to think of two children? To endure the physical and physiological exhaustion of pregnancy and the rest?" (as cited in Hunter-Kilmer).

In 1913, Maria was pregnant for the fourth and final time. When she was four months pregnant with Enrichetta, Maria was diagnosed with placenta previa. She was hemorrhaging, and doctors advised that an abortion along with total bed rest was the best chance of saving Maria's life. Even so, they estimated that her chance of survival was about 5% and counseled Luigi to prepare to become a widower.

Maria and Luigi refused the abortion and put their trust in God's protection. Miraculously, both mother and baby safely survived the pregnancy. Labor was induced early, and a healthy baby girl was born; Maria made a full recovery. After Enrichetta's birth, Luigi's faith greatly increased, and he became as passionate about serving Christ as Maria was.

The Domestic Church

The Quattrocchi household was pious. Maria and Luigi tried to create a domestic church where they could raise children who loved God and each other, too. The family regularly participated in the sacraments, and often attended daily Mass. They also said a daily family Rosary, participated in a First Friday holy hour, and went on periodic weekend retreats. Maria and Luigi also consecrated their home and their family to the Sacred Heart of Jesus.

But their domestic church was joyfully chaotic, too. The family enjoyed playing sports. They took vacations to the ocean or the mountains together. Family dinners were known for being quite lively and famously noisy; the family had the charism of hospitality. They often welcomed others into their home—not just friends, but hungry people they met in the streets as well.

During World War II and the German occupation of Italy, the Quattrocchi family stayed in Rome. They suffered, like everyone else, but trusted in God throughout this difficult time. Maria served as a nurse with the Red Cross, and the family used their apartment to help others, despite living just a few blocks from several government offices. They sheltered refugees and helped smuggle Jewish people out of the city. The family would feed them, disguise them as being part of a Catholic religious order, and send them to an abbey. It's estimated that Maria and Luigi saved about 150 people by sheltering them and smuggling them to safety.

Work Outside the Home

In addition to raising her children, Maria continued her professional work. She wrote for Catholic magazines and authored several books on education and the family, including a book about the role of mothers in their children's education. She worked with a group to help establish the Catholic University of the Sacred Heart. Maria also served as a catechist and volunteered with UNITALSI, an organization that assisted people on pilgrimages to Lourdes.

Maria and Luigi performed good works as a couple, too. They were involved in apostolates promoting marriage and family life, such as assisting young couples through their marriage preparation. They became Third Order Franciscans. And the entire Quattrocchi family helped bring scouting to Italy and formed a scout group for young people from the poorer areas of Rome.

Despite all of the demands on her time, Maria remained devoted to prayer and had a deep, fruitful prayer life. She and Luigi always encouraged their children to take any problem they faced to prayer. They worked hard to help their children understand and appreciate their faith, and the family tried to "outdo" each other in virtue.

Maria and Luigi sought to be holy, but that didn't mean their relationship didn't have its challenges, too. They had disagreements, disappointments, and conflicts, just like any married couple. Maria could be aggressive and overly assertive, while Luigi could be too meek and mild. Maria disapproved of Luigi's smoking habit; he gave it up for a while when their children were young, but picked it back up once the children left home, and this greatly irritated Maria.

Nevertheless, the family, as a whole, was truly devoted to the will of God. Three of their four children eventually entered religious life. Filippo became a diocesan priest, Cesare became a Trappist monk, and Stefania became a Benedictine nun. Maria and Luigi wholeheartedly supported their children's vocations but were still saddened by their departure from family life and felt their absence quite keenly.

After 20 years of marriage, Maria and Luigi took a vow of marital chastity—something that would likely be counseled against today. They desired to give everything to God, no matter how difficult it was. Luigi died in 1951, when the couple had been married for 46 years. Maria lived as a widow for 14 years after his death.

Maria wrote more and volunteered more after Luigi's death. She continued working with UNITALSI and volunteered on the trains that carried disabled people to Lourdes. Maria was also part of an Italian Catholic movement called Movement for a Better World. She died in Enrichetta's arms in 1965.

Their Legacy

Maria and Luigi were beatified together in 2001: the first married couple to be beatified at the same time. Three of their children—Filippo, Cesare, and Enrichetta—were present at the beatification ceremony. Their feast day is their wedding anniversary: November 25. Their daughter Enrichetta has been declared "venerable" by the Church and is also having her cause for canonization examined.

Maria and Luigi truly created a family of saints! As one biographer put it, "They were just a holy couple raising holy kids—the most extraordinary of ordinary callings" (Hunter-Kilmer, 2017). It's true: Getting married and raising a family is a very ordinary calling. But Maria's story shows us that God can make ordinary things a source of extraordinary virtue when we give them into His hands.

In fact, in many ways, it might be easier to be sanctified by a single heroic act than by the small, mundane, tedious actions of daily life. Remaining cheerful and loving while changing a diaper, doing the breakfast dishes, or folding the laundry for the hundredth (or thousandth) time can sometimes take extraordinary grace. For so many of us, though, these small actions are our path to holiness as long as we persevere and try to do them out of love instead of obligation.

Maria's story gives us a beautiful example of the kind of joy-filled household that can arise when we serve our families with great love. Their life wasn't perfect, but it was oriented toward God and trying to live according to His will. As a result, heroic virtue was developed through each small, daily act.

The Quattrocchi home was a wonderful example of the domestic church. The family's faith was strengthened through their participation in family life, and their family life was strengthened through their faith. Maria and Luigi greatly promoted the sacraments and relied on receiving the sacraments as their foundation, together with the family's shared prayer life. But theirs wasn't a domestic church of silence; it was a place of laughter and joy.

Some might take heart in knowing that a home can be filled with laughter instead of silence and still be holy. After all, family life can be chaotic and messy; it's just about impossible to keep a house full of children quiet and still for any length of time. Maria let her children live a real life. They played and had fun; it wasn't all prayer, all the time. And they were still made holy! Maria created an atmosphere in their home that was loving and mindful of God, and the children grew up demonstrating those same qualities.

In fact, Maria gives us a beautiful example of a mother who knew how to balance her work in the domestic church with her work in the professional sphere. She continued to write books and articles after their marriage and after the children were born, even though it was not common during that time for a woman to hold a professional role after marrying and having children. She felt it important to continue to exercise *all* of the gifts that God had given her, not just the maternal ones, and she was able to serve God by pouring her wisdom into others.

Maria's professional work also reveals another way that she and Luigi were united in their line of thinking. He supported her writing and her professional activities, even though social opinion was against a woman like Maria performing that type of work. But Luigi knew it was important to Maria, so it became important to him too.

Maria also found the time and energy to serve others, too. She shows us that it's possible to serve both our families and the world around us, and that our lives will be even richer as a result.

Most deeply, Maria's life shows us great faith and trust. This is probably demonstrated most profoundly in her and Luigi's decision to continue with Enrichetta's pregnancy after the diagnosis of placenta previa. The odds were terribly against her, but Maria put her trust in God anyway. She knew that there was a very strong chance that she would die, and she accepted that possibility because she trusted that God would use whatever happened for His glory.

Of course, that isn't to say that she always had superhuman serenity. Maria was human, just like the rest of us, and she had times when complete trust in God was really, really hard. The couple had three babies in four years, and Maria had mixed emotions about her pregnancies. She was always open to new life but admitted to friends that she felt scared and overwhelmed during the pregnancies.

How important it is to know that we can struggle with what God put in front of us and still accept His plan anyway! In many ways, it makes Maria's story more powerful when we know about her struggles, fears, worries, and the fact that she was still on fire for the Lord anyway. Like Maria, we can have the confidence to move past our doubts and our fears to embrace whatever God has tasked us with, trusting that He'll give us the tools to make it all happen.

By all accounts, Maria's life was pretty normal. She practiced her profession, got married, had babies, and raised her children. But the faith, trust, and sacrifice that she exhibited throughout her life turned into something beautiful. The next time we're feeling disheartened by how mundane and boring our lives seem to be, maybe we can remember Maria Quattrocchi and how God turned her ordinary life into an extraordinary testimony.

Blessed Maria Quattrocchi, pray for us!

Reflection Questions

- It's possible to say that, in some ways, Maria blended serving her family and her community together when she wrote about family life or involved her family in community activities like scouting. Do you find it easier to serve others as a family, a couple, a group of friends, or an individual? Why do you think that is?

- It's written that Maria could be aggressive and bossy at times. How do you handle arguments or conflicts with those close to you? Is prayer in your toolbox?

- What ordinary circumstances and actions in your life might be part of your path to holiness?

Chapter 16:
Gertrud Luckner 1900-1995
Germany

In History

- During and after World War II, a school of economic thought, the *Soziale Marktwirtschaft*, or "social free market," emerged at the University of Freiburg in Germany. Its members believed in free markets and included Walter Euken and Ludwig Erhard. The school opposed the rationing and price controls the Nazis had imposed prior to the war, and which were contributing to runaway inflation and shortages of basic goods like food after the war.

- In 1948, Erhard became the director of the Office of Economic Opportunity and he quickly established new policies. One of his first moves was the creation of a new currency, the Deutsche mark. He also reduced the money supply by 93%, which put an end to the rampant inflation. He also abolished price controls, and these measures began to resolve the issues around the lack of goods available and also absenteeism from work. Absenteeism had become an issue as people needed to spend large amounts of time to find and barter for basic goods.

- West Germany experienced what came to be known as the German Economic Miracle. In only one decade, it had rebuilt so much that industrial production was four times higher than it had been in 1948.

In Society

- In his book *Mainsprings of the German Revival*, Henry Wallich wrote about the effects of Erhard's policies on the people of West Germany, "The spirit of the country changed overnight. The gray, hungry, dead-looking figures wandering about the streets in their everlasting search for food came to life" (p. 71).

- Life in East Germany was very different from that in the West. Under strong Soviet influence, shortages of basic goods persisted, and economic growth stagnated. Civil liberties were curtailed, and thousands of Easterners fled or attempted to flee to the West.

- The fall of the Berlin Wall on November 9, 1989, heralded the end of communist rule in East Germany and much of Eastern Europe. It was a first step towards German reunification and offered new avenues for religious and civil freedom. In 1990, East and West Germany were reunited into one country and the first election was held that all Germans could vote in since before World War II.

I thought: You must always comfort them. The only thing I can do is walk the way together with them.

–Gertrud Luckner

With a bias for action and an international perspective, Gertrud Luckner channeled the terrible cruelty she saw in Germany in the 1930s and 40s to fuel terrific heroism. Starting as a young woman, Gertrud dedicated her whole life to interfaith dialogue and to serving those in need, especially among the Jewish people. Her influence is still felt today, though few might know it.

A Tumultuous Start

Originally born Jane Hartmann in 1900 in Liverpool, England, Gertrud was the only child of German parents. The family moved back to Germany when Gertrud was six years old. Her parents died when she was still quite young, and she was adopted by the Luckner family, who changed her name to Gertrud Luckner. Gertrud was raised by both families as a Quaker but converted to Catholicism later in her life.

Gertrud attended high school in Königsberg, East Prussia. She moved back to England in the 1920s and studied political economy at Woodbrooke, a Quaker college in Birmingham, England. During the summers, she worked and noticed groups of socially and economically disadvantaged people working together to help each other attain a better state in life. This idea greatly attracted her and later became the subject of her doctoral thesis.

She moved back to Germany in 1931 to study at the University of Freiburg, which she chose because the citizens of Freiburg had a reputation for being open-minded. When she got to Freiburg, however, she was alarmed by the Nazi propaganda she encountered and the spreading influence of Nazi ideology.

A Social Activist is Born

Rather than wring her hands, Gertrud took action. She went to the local secondary schools and asked to form discussion groups so that students could practice their English. At the discussion groups, she provided the students with both pro- and anti-Nazi propaganda to read and discuss. Gertrud sparked debates in order to teach the students to think critically about what they were reading.

She kept up on global news by reading the foreign newspapers that the university library threw out each week. Gertrud wanted to know what was *really* going on around her and to keep up with the news that wasn't reported in the German newspapers. She realized the depth and scope of the antisemitism spreading throughout Germany due to Nazi ideology long before most people and saw the threat that it represented.

Gertrud was a pacifist and an early member of the German Catholics' Peace Association, which was later banned by the Nazi party. She supported people who were victims of political persecution as early as 1933 and had a strong interest in working for social welfare. She also converted to Catholicism around this time. Later, in 1938, Gertrud finished her PhD at the University of Freiburg.

The Office for War Relief

After completing her doctorate, Gertrud started working for Caritas—the German Association of Catholic Charitable Organizations—right after the *Kristallnacht* (Night of Broken Glass), a night in November 1938 when the Nazi Party destroyed many synagogues and buildings owned by Jewish people in addition to arresting many Jewish men. Gertrud, with the blessing of Archbishop Conrad Gröber, organized a special "Office for War Relief" within Caritas in 1939. This office, with Gertrud at its head, became the main tool for Catholics in Freiburg to help "non-Aryans," whether they were Jewish or Christian.

As head of the Office for War Relief, Gertrud was able to travel around Germany and Austria to gather information, distribute funds, warn those in danger, and bring news to individual families. She used the information that she had gathered to help Jewish people facing deportation to escape.

Gertrud's personal, international network of contacts was key in her efforts to smuggle Jewish people out of the country over the Swiss border. She relied on the contacts she'd made through her discussion groups, her involvement in the German Catholics Peace Movement, and her friends from England and America—most of whom she'd met while studying in England—to help refugees find shelter abroad.

But smuggling Jewish people out of the country was far from the only way that Gertrud helped people. Her contacts all over Europe and America allowed her to create a sort of underground network that provided financial assistance to Jews, who were increasingly discriminated against and pushed into poverty by Nazi laws.

Gertrud also assisted Jewish families who faced logistical difficulties in the simple task of buying groceries due to Nazi laws. Many Jewish people were forced to work long hours in factories, but they were also restricted to doing their shopping only between 4 p.m. and 6 p.m. each day. That meant that many of them were unable to shop during their designated hours because they were working. So Gertrud organized groups of people who could shop on behalf of the Jewish people working in the factories and deliver groceries to them.

When Gertrud heard rumors about upcoming labor transports, she persuaded a local Freiburg industrialist to say that he couldn't possibly spare the Jewish workers from his factories because more armaments were needed. Thus, the workers were spared from this potential death sentence. She also convinced a few local physicians to admit elderly Jewish people to hospitals so that they couldn't be put on the transports and deported.

After the law was passed that Jewish people had to always wear a Star of David when in public, Gertrud spoke to her parish priest about how to ensure that converted Jewish Catholics would still be able to attend Mass. She organized groups of people to walk with the Jewish Catholics from their homes to Mass (and back) so that they wouldn't be deprived of the opportunity to receive the sacraments.

Gertrud also personally made it a point, when she was out, to go up to people wearing the Star of David and talk to them, even if simply to ask for directions. She wanted to show them that people still saw past the Star of David they were wearing and recognized their human dignity.

Through her position as head of the Office for War Relief, Gertrud was able to get information about people in concentration camps. She collected money, food, and clothing for people in the camps and prisoners of war. Gertrud also worked closely with Rabbi Leo Baeck, the leader of the Reich Union of Jews in Germany, until he was deported to a concentration camp in 1943.

Gertrud's activities flew under the radar for a while, but in 1943, she was eventually arrested by the Gestapo while on her way to Berlin to bring money to the Jews still living there. She was taken to Ravensbrück concentration camp, where she was accused of being a Catholic activist and interrogated for weeks. She spent nearly two years as an inmate at Ravensbrück, barely managing to survive for 19 months until the camp was liberated in 1945.

The Evolution of Gertrud's Ecumenism

After the war, Gertrud organized welfare services in Freiburg and worked tirelessly to aid refugees. She started the *Freiburger Rundbrief*, or the Freiburg Circular, in 1948, dedicated to promoting dialogue and friendship between Jews and Christians. Its mission was stated as "the furtherance of friendship between the people of God's Old and New Covenant, in the spirit of both Testaments" (as cited in Petuchowski). She encouraged people not to give in to the temptation to avoid speaking of what had happened during the Holocaust, and her work indirectly influenced one of the documents that later came out of Vatican II. The document—which condemns antisemitism and persecution of Jewish people, whether occurring in the past or the future—was ratified by the council.

In fact, most of Gertrud's life after the war was focused on promoting ecumenism between Christian people and Jewish people. She was invited to Israel in 1951 by her friend Rabbi Leo Baeck, becoming one of the first German citizens to visit Israel. Yad Vashem recognized Gertrud as "Righteous Among the Nations" in 1966, and she received various honors from the German government: the Buber-Rosenzweig Medal in 1980 and the Sir Sigmund-Sternberg Prize in 1987. A retirement home for women that was founded to specifically serve Christians who had escaped the Nazis was also named for her.

Gertrud died in 1995 and was an advocate of Jewish–Christian dialogue up to the end of her life. She never viewed her work during the war as extraordinary and always said it was "obvious" why she did what she did; she was treating people with the human dignity that they deserved.

The Power of a Personal Connection

Gertrud fought persecution and discrimination first and foremost by treating people as people. She knew that racism and antisemitism reduced people from human beings to things, so she fought back very simply: she emphasized their humanity.

Gertrud also emphasized that her relief efforts and her social welfare work depended upon person-to-person interaction. She approached things not from an institutional perspective, but from a personal one. In fact, Gertrud believed that a person-to-person connection was the best way to fight a dictatorship because dictators couldn't or wouldn't understand that type of relationship.

This interrelatedness wasn't limited to only people who shared her ethnicity, nationality, or faith. Gertrud believed in crossing boundaries to form bonds across all aspects of society. Her Catholic faith spurred her to a sense of universality; Gertrud truly recognized the body of Christ as a global, all-inclusive body.

Gertrud's entire life witnessed her inclusive recognition of all people as dignified children of God. Her visits to Jewish people in the ghettos, her public acknowledgment of people wearing the Star of David, and her work to improve relationships between Christians and Jews are all evidence of this.

Gertrud had real concern for the everyday issues that people faced. Although she was highly educated, she wasn't interested in only talking about theoretical ideas. Instead, she was busy coming up with practical solutions to the individual problems at hand. Gertrud didn't talk; she acted. She looked at the person in front of her, assessed their problem, and then used her connections and knowledge to address that specific problem. Everything that she did was on a very intimate, personal level.

In many ways, her treatment of people as individuals to be served imitates how Jesus served people during his earthly ministry. Like Jesus, Gertrud didn't wait to look for a pattern of problems and then set up an organization dedicated to addressing the pattern. Instead, she took each person's problem and then took the necessary steps to address it.

One anecdote from her work during the Nazi persecution particularly illustrates this: Gertrud learned of two elderly Jewish women who were afraid to be alone in their house at night because of the Nazis. So, she went to their home and stayed with them every night for three weeks until she could arrange for them to escape. Gertrud didn't contact an organization, ask for permission, or debate about what to do. She just heard their problem and acted on it.

Gertrud's ability to take action in some ways stemmed from how she worked. Her ministry to the Jewish people was personal, whether official or unofficial. It often depended on her network of personal contacts rather than a diplomatic or social institution. Although Gertrud worked for Caritas and utilized her role with the Office for War Relief to aid people, she often acted alone and unofficially. While she was driven to act by her faith, she worked both inside and outside of its formal institutions to serve people.

Her dedication to service meant that Gertrud wasn't afraid to stand up in the face of persecution. She chose not to worry about the risk to herself; instead, she focused on the people who needed help. Gertrud walked with them; she didn't want them to feel alone and abandoned. Even when she was arrested and taken to Ravensbrück, she focused on what she *could* do rather than the dangers she faced. She tried comforting the people around her and reminding them they were walking together.

Gertrud was an ecumenist long before ecumenism was a focal point in the Church. Her efforts to create a bridge between Christians and Jews might have been "unofficial," but they were certainly effective. She focused on similarities rather than differences and encouraged people to keep talking to each other at a person-to-person level.

She may not have seen her social welfare efforts as extraordinary, but through her actions, many people were saved from the Nazis and had their human dignity restored. We might not be in a situation to save people from concentration camps, but like Gertrud, we can fight racism and discrimination by seeing the human dignity inherent in every person. We can work to make person-to-person connections, and we can stand firm in doing what we know is right.

Gertrud Luckner, pray for us!

Reflection Questions

- Gertrud understood well the value of personal relationships. Who are the people you rely on for help in your spiritual journey? In daily life? Who relies on you?

- Gertrud lost her parents not once but twice. She also lost many friends throughout World War II and her long life. Despite this, she continued to serve. How has loss impacted your approach to faith and to life?

- The goal of life is to grow in love of God and others. What small actions can you take today or this week to show your love for someone and/or honor their dignity?

Conclusion

The women whose lives are chronicled here acted with courage and purpose during their everyday lives. They sought out the voice of God and followed His calling to serve others. Their stories are all unique and remind us that no two paths to holiness are the same. Yet, they all shared a commitment to pursuing the Lord with boldness and a determination to give witness to the Gospel by making life better in some way for those around them.

Dorothy Day tirelessly championed Catholic social teaching and used her gifts as a journalist to spread awareness of the challenges faced by the working poor. She also balanced her responsibilities as a mother with her responsibilities as a working professional. Margit Slachta was both a politician and a nun who courageously defended human dignity; she served in Parliament and started a religious order that saved huge numbers of Jewish people during the Holocaust.

Mother Teresa saw the face of Christ in each person that she helped from the street, and inspired the world with her radical love and service, despite not feeling God's presence for much of her ministry. She showed us that greatness can be achieved in small, seemingly insignificant steps. Sofía del Valle championed women's education and workers' rights and became a bridge between Catholicism in Mexico and the rest of the world, reminding people that you can serve the Church brilliantly as a laywoman. Edith Stein's theological writings have inspired thousands; she also willingly embraced the Cross as the instrument of salvation and in doing so, further inspired us with her openness to sacrifice.

Thea Bowman joyously showed every person and every community she encountered that they are loved by God. She brought together her identity as a Catholic and an African American to remind the people around her that there is no one single way to "look" or "act" Catholic. Gianna Beretta Molla loved God and her family deeply. She joyfully embraced sacrifice as part of her vocation to motherhood and saw loving her family as a path to heaven. Cory Aquino trusted God amid conflict and rallied an entire nation behind her to fight an unjust authoritarian leader. M. Madeleva Wolff opened doors for women to learn advanced theology and participate in the theological life of the Church.

Anuarite Nengapeta was ready to face extreme physical danger for the sake of her faith; she relied on God to give her strength. Margarete Sommer risked her life to save Jewish people from the Nazis and called for the Church to speak out against antisemitism. Boleslawa Lament worked for ecumenism and founded a religious order to help serve others. Daphrose Rugamba witnessed the incredible impact that deep faith can have on a family; she advocated for peace between different ethnic groups and formed communities that deepened people's faith.

Irmã Dulce Lopes Pontes served the poor one person at a time by treating each as an individual and meeting his or her needs in the moment. Maria Quattrocchi showed us that holiness can be achieved in everyday moments and that creating a domestic church can leave a family legacy of service to God. Finally, Gertrud Luckner fought antisemitism, risked her own safety to serve Jews during the Holocaust, and later devoted herself to bridging the divide between Christians and Jews.

Sixteen women, sixteen unique stories. Some of them are canonized saints or are on the path to canonization, while others have not been formally recognized by the Church. But every one of them loved God, and they loved others.

It's my hope that you have found at least one woman within these pages whose story resonates with you and your particular circumstances in life. They cover a wide range of charisms and vocations, and every one of them served God differently. They show us that following God and living a life of holiness can take any number of forms.

I hope that you feel energized and emboldened to embrace your own sacred calling in life. Remember that each of us has our own path to holiness, and when we perform small, everyday actions with great love, we transform them into something extraordinary. Each of us has our own vocation, and our responsibilities within that vocation aren't obstacles to incredible holiness. Instead, they're the vehicle by which we can obtain it. We don't have to move a mountain to show people our faith. Our daily acts of holiness—helping a neighbor, wiping a nose, cooking a meal, doing our work well, teaching others about the love of Christ, praying with or for someone in need—add up to a powerful testimony of faith over time.

So, embrace your own vocation, whatever that looks like, and lean into the way that God has called you to love and serve. **Let's go out and change the world by boldly pursuing holiness in our everyday actions and by allowing God to transform our lives, one small act at a time!**

References

1898-1933: America's Colony. (n.d.) Frontline World. https://www.pbs.org/frontlineworld/stories/philippines/tl 01.html. Accessed April 2024.

1903 Wright Flyer. (n.d.) National Air and Space Museum. https://airandspace.si.edu/collection-objects/1903-wright-flyer/nasm_A19610048000. Accessed February 2024.

1934-1964: War and Independence. (n.d.) Frontline World. https://www.pbs.org/frontlineworld/stories/philippines/tl 02.html. Accessed April 2024.

1950s. (n.d.) Barbie Media. https://www.barbiemedia.com/timeline.html. Accessed February 2024.

19th-20th c. Colonialism & Resistance. (N.d.) Pardee School of Global Studies. https://www.bu.edu/africa/outreach/teachingresources/history/colonialism/. Accessed February 2024.

2023 student awards. (n.d.). Center for Social Concerns. https://socialconcerns.nd.edu/2023-student-awards/. Accessed February 2024.

About Catholic Charismatic Renewal. (n.d.) Catholic Charismatic Renewal National Service Committee. https://www.nsc-chariscenter.org/about-ccr/. Accessed February 2024.

About Saint John Paul II. (n.d.) Saint John Paul II National Shrine. https://www.jp2shrine.org/en/about/jp2bio.html. Accessed February 2024.

About UNESCO Mexico. (n.d.). UNESCO. https://www.unesco.org/en/fieldoffice/mexico. Accessed January 2024.

Alexander, K. L. (2019). *Corazon Aquino.* National Women's History Museum. https://www.womenshistory.org/education-resources/biographies/corazon-aquino. Accessed April 2024.

Allaire, J. & Broughton, R. (1995). *Praying with Dorothy Day.* Word Among Us Press.

Allen, E. (2023, February 1). *Congo Catholics urge sainthood for two beloved martyrs*. Crux. https://cruxnow.com/pope-in-south-sudan-congo/2023/02/congo-catholics-urge-sainthood-for-two-beloved-martyrs. Accessed February 2024.

Andes, S. (2019). *The Mysterious Sofía: One woman's mission to save Catholicism in twentieth-century Mexico*. University of Nebraska Press.

Angel of Mercy: The story of Sister Margaret Slachta. (n.d.). ZALA Films. http://www.zalafilms.com/films/angelofmercy.html. Accessed September 2023.

Barron, R. (2020, January 27). *"1917", War, and Faith* [Video]. YouTube. https://www.youtube.com/watch?v=5tSD3-96yE8. Accessed February 2024.

Barron, R. (2019, October 3). *Bishop Barron on His Theological Path* [Video]. YouTube. https://www.youtube.com/watch?v=QB6w4miLEc8. Accessed February 2024.

Benito Mussolini. (2024, January 21). Britannica. https://www.britannica.com/biography/Benito-Mussolini/Rise-to-power. Accessed February 2024.

Bennett, C. (2021, May 23). *Cyprien and Daphrose Rugamba, Servants of God*. Holier Matrimony. https://holiermatrimony.com/?p=259. Accessed September 2023.

Beutner, D. (2021, November 25). *Living "an ordinary life in an extraordinary way."* The Catholic World Report. https://www.catholicworldreport.com/2021/11/25/living-an-ordinary-life-in-an-extraordinary-way-blesseds-luigi-beltrame-quattrochi-and-maria-corsini/. Accessed February 2024.

Bhalla, G. (2022, Summer). *The Story of the 1947 Partition as Told by the People Who Were There*. HUMANITIES, 43(3). https://www.neh.gov/article/story-1947-partition-told-people-who-were-there. Accessed April 2024.

Biography. (n.d.). Sister Thea Bowman Cause for Canonization.

https://www.sistertheabowman.com/biography/.
Accessed October 2023.

Biography of St. Pius X. (n.d.) Church of St. Pius X.
https://saintpiusxchurch.com/wp/sample-page/about-
us/biography-of-st-pius-x/. Accessed February 2024.

Blessed Alphonsine Anuarite Nengapeta. (2023, July 1).
CatholicSaintsInfo. http://catholicsaints.info/blessed-
alphonsine-anuarite-nengapeta/. Accessed October
2023.

Blessed Boleslawa Maria Lament. (2023, July 3).
CatholicSaintsInfo. http://catholicsaints.info/blessed-
boleslawa-maria-lament/. Accessed October 2023.

Breslin, C. (2016, February 2). Catholic heroes... Blessed
Boleslava Maria Lament. *The Wanderer Online Daily.*
https://thewandererpress.com/saints/catholic-heroes-
blessed-boleslava-maria-lament/. Accessed October
2023.

Brief History. (n.d.) The Embassy of the Republic of Rwanda,
Washington D.C. USA.
https://rwandaembassy.org/about-rwanda. Accessed
February 2024.

Brockhaus, H. (2019, May 14). *Woman who served Brazil's
poorest to be canonized.* Catholic News Agency.
https://www.catholicnewsagency.com/news/41279/wo
man-who-served-brazils-poorest-to-be-canonized.
Accessed October 2023.

Buchholz, K. (2019, August 15). *When Did U.S. States
Become States?* Statista.
https://www.statista.com/chart/19038/dates-of-
statehood-us/. Accessed February 2024.

Burger, J. (2021, December 12). *How Pope John Paul II
contributed to the fall of Soviet communism.* Aleteia.
https://aleteia.org/2021/12/23/how-pope-john-paul-ii-
contributed-to-the-fall-of-soviet-communism/.
Accessed February 2024.

Burns, P. (2003). *Butler's lives of the saints: New concise
edition.* Liturgical Press.

Caplow, T, L. Hicks, B. Wattenberg. "The First Measured
 Century: An Illustrated Guide to Trends in America,
 1900–2000." AEI Press.

CAPP-USA. (N.d.) *The Origin of Catholic Social Teaching: The
 Church's Best Kept Secret.* Catholic Social Teaching
 in Action. https://capp-usa.org/2021/03/catholic-social-
 teaching-origin/. Accessed February 2024.

Catholic Church. (2000). *Catechism of the Catholic Church:
 revised in accordance with the official Latin text
 promulgated by Pope John Paul II.* United States
 Catholic Conference.

*Catholic nun, first female MP, and Rightous Among the
 Nations, Margit Slachta, reburied in Budapest.* (2021,
 December 8). Hungary Today.
 https://hungarytoday.hu/catholic-nun-first-female-mp-
 righteous-among-nations-jews-ww2-margit-slachta/.
 Accessed September 2023.

Cep, C. (2020, April 6). *Dorothy Day's Radical Faith.* The New
 Yorker.
 https://www.newyorker.com/magazine/2020/04/13/dor
 othy-days-radical-faith. Accessed September 2023.

Civil Rights Movement Timeline. (January 24, 2024). History.
 https://www.history.com/topics/black-history/civil-
 rights-movement-timeline. Accessed February 2024.

Cline, Austin. (2020, August 28). *Popes of the 20th Century.*
 https://www.learnreligions.com/popes-of-the-20th-
 century-250632. Accessed February 2024.

Coppen, L. (2022, August 8). *'Doctor of resilient hope' - the
 last days of Edith Stein.* The Pillar.
 https://www.pillarcatholic.com/p/doctor-of-resilient-
 hope-the-last. Accessed September 2023.

Corazon Aquino biography. (2021, April 19). Biography.com.
 https://www.biography.com/political-figures/corazon-
 aquino. Accessed September 2023.

Corazon Aquino quotes. (n.d.). BrainyQuote. Retrieved
 October 13, 2023, from
 https://www.brainyquote.com/quotes/corazon_aquino_
 201108. Accessed September 2023.

Crisostomo, I. T. (1987). *Cory: Profile of a president.* Branden Publishing Company.

Crossin, J. (2012, Fall). *The Ecumenical Movement: A School for Virtue.* United States Conference of Catholic Bishops. https://www.usccb.org/committees/ecumenical-interreligious-affairs/vatican-ii-and-ecumenical-movement. Accessed February 2024.

Cyprien and Daphrose Rugamba. (n.d.). Emmanuel Community. https://emmanuel.info/en/cyprien-and-daphrose-rugamba-their-story/. Accessed October 2023.

Cyprien and Daphrose Rugamba - The Battle of Love. (2021, April 7). Emmanuel Community. https://emmanuel.info/en/cyprian-and-daphrose-rugamba-the-battle-of-love/. Accessed October 2023.

Danis, J. (2023). *The story of Cyprien and Daphrose Rugamba.* The Word Among Us. https://wau.org/archives/article/a_grace_that_conquers_all/. Accessed October 2023.

D'Emilio, F. (2022, September 1). *'Crushed' by 2 papacies, John Paul I's death eclipsed life.* AP News. https://apnews.com/article/religion-vatican-city-de1abd9874700be75f2420bd57e991f7. Accessed February 2024.

Demographic Trends. (n.d.) Britannica. https://www.britannica.com/place/Philippines/Demographic-trends. Accessed April 2024.

Depaepe, M and Angotako Mawanzo, D. (N.d.) *Colonial Education in the Belgian Congo.* Sorbonne Universite. https://ehne.fr/en/encyclopedia/themes/education-teaching-and-professional-training/education-in-a-colonial-environment/colonial-education-in-belgian-congo. Accessed April 2024.

Donnelly, M. Q. (1990, April 28). *Sister Thea Bowman (1937-1990): From April 28, 2990.* America: The Jesuit Review.

https://www.americamagazine.org/issue/100/sister-thea-bowman-1937-1990. Accessed September 2023.

Dorothy Day - A saint for our times. (n.d.). U.S. Catholic. https://uscatholic.org/dorothy-day-a-saint-for-our-times/. Accessed September 2023.

Dorothy Day quotes. (n.d.). BrainyQuote. https://www.brainyquote.com/quotes/dorothy_day_316 242. Accessed September 2023.

Editors of the Encyclopedia Britannica. *Belgian Congo.* (2024, May 31) Britannica. https://www.britannica.com/place/Belgian-Congo. Accessed July 7, 2024. Accessed May 2024.

Elkens, T. and Berentsen, W. (2024, June 19) *Germany.* Britannica. https://www.britannica.com/place/Germany. Accessed May 2024.

Experimentation with Sound. (n.d.) MoMA. https://www.moma.org/collection/terms/film/experiment ation-with-sound. Accessed February 2024.

Explore WWII History. (n.d.) The National World War II Museum. https://www.nationalww2museum.org/students-teachers/student-resources/explore-wwii-history. Accessed February 2024.

Flappers. (February 12, 2024). History. https://www.history.com/topics/roaring-twenties/flappers. Accessed February 2024.

Fox, T. (2016, January 7). *Sr. Madaleva Wolff forever changed the face of Catholic theology.* Global Sisters Report. https://www.globalsistersreport.org/news/trends/sr-madaleva-wolff-forever-changed-face-catholic-theology-36166. Accessed September 2023.

From War to War in Europe: 1919-1939. (2018, May 24). National WWII Museum. https://www.nationalww2museum.org/war/articles/war-war-europe-1919-1939. Accessed February 2024.

Gajanan, M. (2016, September 2). *A brief history of Mother Teresa's complicated faith.* Time.

https://time.com/4476076/mother-teresas-faith-history/. Accessed September 2023.

Geernaert, D. (2020, July 28). *Changes in Catholic approaches to ecumenism.* SL Media. https://slmedia.org/blog/one-body-changes-in-catholic-approaches-to-ecumenism. Accessed February 2024.

Germany before World War I. (n.d.). Alpha History. https://alphahistory.com/worldwar1/germany/. Accessed May 2024.

Gertrud Luckner. (n.d.-a). Gedenkstätte Deutscher Widerstand. https://www.gdw-berlin.de/en/recess/biographies/index_of_persons/biographie/view-bio/gertrud-luckner/. Accessed October 2023.

Gertrud Luckner. (n.d.-b). JesusSkeptic. https://www.jesusskeptic.com/humanrights-luckner. Accessed October 2023.

Gertrud Luckner. (n.d.-c). Pax Christi. https://paxchristi.org.uk/resources/peace-people-2/gertrud-luckner/. Accessed October 2023.

Gertrud Luckner. (n.d.-d). Yad Vashem: The World Holocaust Remembrance Center. https://www.yadvashem.org/righteous/stories/luckner.html. Accessed October 2023.

Gethard, G. (2023, August 30). *The German Economic Miracle Post WWII.* Investopedia. https://www.investopedia.com/articles/economics/09/german-economic-miracle.asp. Accessed May 2024.

Glicksman, K. (2019, August 8). *All about Blessed Dulce Lopes Pontes - the good angel of Brazil.* SL Media. https://slmedia.org/blog/all-about-blessed-dulce-lopes-pontes-the-good-angel-of-brazil. Accessed October 2023.

Grennan Gary, H. (2022, Spring). *How We Lived | The Best Science.* In Trust. https://www.intrust.org/in-trust-magazine/issues/spring-2022/how-we-lived. Accessed March 2024.

Harrington, S. (2015, March 14). *The Philippine Normal School During U.S. Colonial Rule, 1901-1916*. Bridgewater State University. https://vc.bridgew.edu/arc_conf/Mar2015/schedule/7/. Accessed April 2024.

Haskins, J. (1988). *Corazon Aquino: Leader of the Philippines*. Enslow Publishers.

Helga. (2017, March 14). *Life in Italy from 1945-1950*. Life In Italy. https://lifeinitaly.com/italy-1945-to-1950/. Accessed April 2024.

Henderson, D. (n.d.). *German Economic Miracle*. Econlib. https://www.econlib.org/library/Enc/GermanEconomic Miracle.html. Accessed April 2024.

Hennessy, K. (2017). *Dorothy Day*, The World Will Be Saved by Beauty. Scribner.

Hernandez, C. and Borlaza, G. (2024, May 28). *History of the Philippines*. https://www.britannica.com/topic/history-of-Philippines/World-War-II. Accessed July 2024.

History. (n.d.). Xavier University of Louisiana. https://www.xula.edu/ibcs/history1.html. Accessed April 2024.

History of the Democratic Republic of the Congo. (n.d.) Britannica. https://www.britannica.com/place/Democratic-Republic-of-the-Congo/History. Accessed April 2024.

History of UNESCO. (n.d.). UNESCO. https://www.unesco.org/en/history. Accessed February 2024.

History.com Editors. (2023, November 16). *Berlin Wall*. History. https://www.history.com/topics/cold-war/berlin-wall. Accessed June 2024.

History.com Editors. (2019, June 6). *Mahatma Gandhi*. History. https://www.history.com/topics/asian-history/mahatma-gandhi. Accessed April 2024.

History.com Editors. (2024, March 27) *Russian Revolution*. History. https://www.history.com/topics/european-history/russian-revolution. Accessed April 2024.

Home. (n.d.). The Dorothy Day Guild. http://dorothydayguild.org/. Accessed September 2023.

How Does Someone Become a Saint? (n.d.) Catholic Answers Shop. https://shop.catholic.com/blog/how-does-someone-become-a-saint-/. Accessed July 11, 2024. Accessed July 2024.

Hubert, M. (2018, June 27). *Hungarian 'Angel of Mercy' champion of human rights.* Western New York Catholic. http://www.wnycatholicarchive.org/news/article/current/2018/06/27/103179/hungarian-angel-of-mercy-champion-of-human-rights. Accessed October 2023.

Hunter-Kilmer, M. (2017, November 25). *Blessed Luigi and Maria Quattrocchi: Ordinary married life, shot through with glory.* Aleteia. https://aleteia.org/2017/11/25/blessed-luigi-and-maria-quattrocchi-ordinary-married-life-shot-through-with-glory/. Accessed October 2023.

Iron Curtain. (February 2, 2024). Britannica. https://www.britannica.com/topic/Radio-Free-Europe. Accessed April 2024.

Jauer, J. & Bost, B. (2015, July 5). *Two human rescuers.* Christ in der Gegenwart. https://www.herder.de/cig/geistesleben/2015/07-12-2015/pater-paul-cahensly-und-margarete-sommer-zwei-menschenretter/. Accessed October 2023.

Joan of Arc's Quote. (n.d.) Maid of Heaven. http://www.maidofheaven.com/joanofarc_quote_I_am_not_afraid.asp. Accessed December 2023.

Jones, K. (1999). *Women saints: Lives of faith and courage.* Orbis Books.

July 4, 1946: The Philippines Gained Independence from the United States. (2021, July 2). National World War II Museum. https://www.nationalww2museum.org/war/articles/july-4-1946-philippines-independence. Accessed April 2024.

Kachroo-Levine, M. (2021, July 20). *What Travel Looked Like Through the Decades.* Travel + Leisure. https://www.travelandleisure.com/travel-tips/what-travel-looked-like-decades. Accessed April 2024.

Keep, J. (2024, May 14). *Nicholas II Tsar of Russia.* Britannica. https://www.britannica.com/biography/Nicholas-II-tsar-of-Russia. Accessed April 2024.

Kenneally, J. (1990). *The History of American Catholic women.* The Crossroad Publishing Company.

Klein, C. *A Timeline of U.S. Anti-War Movements.* (May 19, 2021). https://www.history.com/news/anti-war-movements-throughout-american-history. Accessed April 2024.

Klein, H. and Luna, F. (2019, October 30). *Economy in Brazil in the 20th Century.* Oxford Research Encyclopedias. https://oxfordre.com/latinamericanhistory/display/10.1093/acrefore/9780199366439.001.0001/acrefore-9780199366439-e-833?d. Accessed June 2024.

Koenig-Bricker, W. & Elliott, K. (2020, June). *The married way to holiness.* The Word Among Us. https://wau.org/archives/article/the_married_way_to_holiness/. Accessed October 2023.

Kulik, R. *Eastern bloc.* (n.d.) Britannica. https://www.britannica.com/topic/Eastern-bloc. Accessed February 2024.

Lantz, B. (2023, May 8). *Historical reformer: Dorothy Day.* Nations. https://nations.co/historical-reformer-dorothy-day/. Accessed September 2023.

Lázár, G. (2015, July 30). *Angel of Mercy in Canada - A film about Sister Margit Slachta.* Hungarian Free Press. https://hungarianfreepress.com/2015/07/30/angel-of-mercy-in-canada-a-film-about-sister-margit-slachta/. Accessed September 2023.

Leopold II. King of Belgium. (N.d.) Britannica. https://ehne.fr/en/encyclopedia/themes/education-teaching-and-professional-training/education-in-a-colonial-environment/colonial-education-in-belgian-congo. Accessed April 2024.

L'Osservatore Romano. (2001, October 10). Bl Luigi Beltrame Quattrocchi and Bl. Maria Corsini. EWTN. https://www.ewtn.com/catholicism/library/bl-luigi-beltrame-quattrocchi-and-bl-maria-corsini-5630. Accessed October 2023.

Lovett, C. and Marino, J. (2024, June 15). *Italy*. Britannica. https://www.britannica.com/place/Italy. Accessed April 2024.

Ludwig, T. (n.d.). *Dorothy Day*. Learning to Give. https://www.learningtogive.org/resources/dorothy-day. Accessed September 2023.

Luigi and Maria Beltrame Quattrocchi. (n.d.). RCL Benziger. http://saintsresource.com/luigi-and-maria-beltrame-quattrocchi. Accessed October 2023.

Major documents of Vatican II. (2012, September 11). U.S. Catholic. https://uscatholic.org/articles/201209/major-documents-of-vatican-ii/. Accessed February 2024.

Mandell, G.P. (2010). Madeleva Wolff, C.S.C.: Woman of faith and vision. In T. Groome & M. Daley (Eds.), *Reclaiming Catholicism: Treasures old and new* (pp. 88-92). Orbis Books.

Margarete Sommer. (n.d.-a). Gedenkstätte Deutscher Widerstand. https://www.gdw-berlin.de/en/recess/biographies/index_of_persons/biographie/view-bio/margarete-sommer. Accessed November 2023.

Margarete Sommer. (n.d.-b). Prenzlauer Berg Ecumenical Working Group. https://oeak.de/okumenische-projekte/zeugen-gottes-in-berlin/margarete-sommer/. Accessed November 2023.

Martin Luther King Jr. Biographical. (n.d.) The Nobel Prize. https://www.nobelprize.org/prizes/peace/1964/king/biographical/. Accessed February 2024.

Martins, L. and Schneider, R. (2024, June 3). *Brazil*. Britannica. https://www.britannica.com/place/Brazil. Accessed April 2024.

Matthias, M. (2024, Jan. 30). *St. Pius X.* Britannica. https://www.britannica.com/biography/Saint-Pius-X. Accessed February 2024.

McBrien, R. (2010, August 9). *Popes of the 20th Century.* National Catholic Reporter. https://www.ncronline.org/blogs/essays-theology/popes-20th-century. Accessed February 2024.

McBrien, R. (2010, August 17). *Popes of the 20th Century: John XXIII.* National Catholic Reporter. https://www.ncronline.org/blogs/essays-theology/popes-20th-century-john-xxiii. Accessed February 2024.

McBrien, R. (2010, August 23). *Popes of the 20th Century: Paul VI.* National Catholic Reporter. https://www.ncronline.org/blogs/essays-theology/popes-20th-century-paul-vi. Accessed February 2024.

McGuire, J. (2019, April 26). *7 Basic Points: A Humanae Vitae Summary.* Human Life International. https://www.hli.org/resources/7-basic-points-humanae-vitae-summary/. Accessed February 2024.

McNamara, R. (2021, February 16). *Biography of Dorothy Day, founder of the Catholic Worker movement.* ThoughtCo. https://www.thoughtco.com/dorothy-day-biography-4154465. Accessed October 2023.

McNeill, W. (2005, Fall). *Asia in the Twentieth Century.* Association for Asian Studies. https://www.asianstudies.org/publications/eaa/archives/asia-in-the-twentieth-century/. Accessed February 2024.

McSteen, M. *Fifty Years of Social Security.* (n.d.) Social Security Administration. https://www.ssa.gov/history/50mm2.html. Accessed February 2024.

Meert, C. (2021, October 27). *Saintly parents inspire holy children: Blessed Luigi and Maria Beltrame Quattrocchi.* Agape Catholic Ministries.

https://agapecatholicministries.info/family-life/saintly-parents-inspire-holy-children-blessed-luigi-and-maria-beltrame-quattrocchi/ Accessed October 2023.

Miller, J. (n.d.) *Religion in the Philippines.* Asia Society. https://asiasociety.org/education/religion-philippines. Accessed April 2024.

Mingardi, A. (2021, October 30). *Remembering Luigi Einaudi and the Italian Economic Miracle.* Econlib. https://www.econlib.org/remembering-luigi-einaudi-and-the-italian-economic-miracle/. Accessed May 2024.

Mother Foundress: Life. (n.d.). Missionary Sisters of the Holy Family. http://www.misjonarki-swietej-rodziny.org/en/zalozycielka_zycie.html. Accessed September 2023.

Mother Teresa biography. (2020, February 24). Biography.com. https://www.biography.com/religious-figures/mother-teresa. Accessed September 2023.

Mother Teresa of Calcutta. (n.d.). Catholic Online. https://www.catholic.org/clife/teresa/. Accessed September 2023.

NCS Blog. (2024, March 8). *Recognizing the Tremendous Strides Women Have Made in Higher Education.* National Student Clearinghouse. https://www.studentclearinghouse.org/nscblog/recognizing-the-tremendous-strides-women-have-made-in-higher-education/. Accessed May 2024.

Nervo Codato, A. (2006). *A political history of the Brazilian transition from military dictatorship to democracy.* Universidade Federal do Paraná. Rev. Sociol. Polit. vol.2 no.se Curitiba 2006. chrome-extension://efaidnbmnnnibpcajpcglclefindmkaj/http://socialsciences.scielo.org/pdf/s_rsocp/v2nse/scs_a04.pdf. Accessed April 2024.

Nielsen, E. (2023, January 28). *Sister Thea Bowman (1937 – 1990).* BlackPast. https://www.blackpast.org/african-american-history/thea-bowman-1937-1990/. Accessed September 2023.

Olver, R. (2019, November 8). *What Was It Like Living In Cold War East Germany?* Forces Net. https://www.forces.net/news/what-was-it-living-cold-war-east-germany. Accessed June 2024.

Our history. (n.d.). Missionaries of Charity. https://missionariesofcharity.org/our-history-read-more.html. Accessed September 2023.

Our Lady of Fatima. (n.d.) EWTN. https://www.ewtn.com/catholicism/saints/our-lady-of-fatima-423. Accessed May 2024.

Pettiti, G. (2009, July 19). *Blessed Boleslava Maria Lament.* Santi Beati. https://www.santiebeati.it/dettaglio/92535. Accessed October 2023.

Petuchowski, E. (1999). Gertrud Luckner: Resistance and assistance, a German woman who defied Nazis and aided Jews. In L. Frizzell, (Ed.), *Ministers of Compassion During the Nazi Period: Gertrud Luckner & Raoul Wallenberg* (pp. 4-19). The Institute of Judeo-Christian Studies. https://scholarship.shu.edu/cgi/viewcontent.cgi?article=1002&context=teshuvah-institute-papers. Accessed November 2023.

Phayer, M. (1995, August 18). *Saving Jews was her passion.* Commonweal. https://www.commonwealmagazine.org/saving-jews-was-her-passion. Accessed October 2023.

Phayer, M. & Fleischner, E. (1997). *Cries in the night: Women who challenged the Holocaust.* Sheed & Ward.

Pratt, T. N. (2022, March 16). *Why Pew's new study on Black Catholicism is critical for U.S. church leaders.* National Catholic Reporter. https://www.ncronline.org/news/opinion/why-pews-new-study-black-catholicism-critical-us-church-leaders. Accessed March 2024.

Price, D. *Unemployment Insurance, Then and Now, 1935-85.* (October 1985). Social Security Bulletin, Vol. 48, No. 10.

https://www.ssa.gov/policy/docs/ssb/v48n10/v48n10p2
2.pdf. Accessed February 2024.

A quote by Mother Teresa. (n.d.). Goodreads.
https://www.goodreads.com/quotes/6946-not-all-of-us-can-do-great-things-but-we. Accessed September
2023.

Raviele K, Fehring RJ, Smith J, Linacre Q. *The Catholic
Medical Association and Humanae Vitae: On the
Fiftieth Anniversary of the Encyclical.* 2018
Nov;85(4):311–2. doi: 10.1177/0024363918816677.
Epub 2019 Jan 3. PMCID: PMC6322119. Accessed
February 2024.

Remembering Gertrud Luckner, a singular rescuer. (2020,
August 31). The International Raoul Wallenberg
Foundation.
https://www.raoulwallenberg.net/general/remembering
-gertrud-luckner-a-singular-rescuer/. Accessed
October 2023.

Rerum Novarum – 2 Minute Summary. (n.d.) Christian
Apostles. https://christianapostles.com/rerum-novarum-2-minute-summary/. Accessed February
2024.

Reveal, J. (n.d.). *Madeleva, Sister Mary* (1887-1964).
Encyclopedia.com.
https://www.encyclopedia.com/women/encyclopedias-almanacs-transcripts-and-maps/madeleva-sister-mary-1887-1964. Accessed February 2024.

Rigney, M. (2020, May 18). *Turning empathy into action.*
Minute Meditations.
https://www.franciscanmedia.org/minute-meditations/turning-empathy-into-action/. Accessed
November 2023.

Ripatrazone, N. (2023). *The habit of poetry: The literary lives
of nuns in mid-century America.* Fortress Press.

Saint Gianna Beretta Molla. (2022, April 19). Franciscan
Media. https://www.franciscanmedia.org/saint-of-the-day/saint-gianna-beretta-molla/. Accessed November
2023.

Saro, N. S. (2021, October 13). *Reflection: Rwandan martyrs Cyprien and Daphrose Rugamba modeled pacifism, prayer.* Black Catholic Messenger. https://www.blackcatholicmessenger.com/rugamba-martyrs-reflection/. Accessed November 2023.

Sarr, L. (2021, September 29). *Family killed in Rwandan genocide on track to sainthood.* LaCroix International. https://international.la-croix.com/news/religion/family-killed-in-rwandan-genocide-on-track-to-sainthood/14964. Accessed November 2023.

Second Vatican Council. (2024, February 22). Britannica. https://www.britannica.com/event/Second-Vatican-Council. Accessed February 2024.

Seven Themes of Catholic Social Teaching. (2005). United States Conference of Catholic Bishops. https://www.usccb.org/beliefs-and-teachings/what-we-believe/catholic-social-teaching/seven-themes-of-catholic-social-teaching. Accessed February 2024.

Sheetz, J. (n.d.). *Margit Slachta and the early rescue of Jewish families, 1939-42.* Millersville University. https://www.millersville.edu/holocon/files/margit-slachta-and-the-early-rescue-of-jewish-families.pdf. Accessed September 2023.

Sheetz-Nguyen, J. (2001). Transcending boundaries: Hungarian Roman Catholic religious women and the "persecuted ones." In O. Bartov & P. Mack (Eds.), *In God's name: Genocide and religion in the twentieth century* (pp. 222-242). Berghahn Books.

Sister M. Madaleva Wolff. (n.d.). Michiana Women Leaders. https://www.michianawomenleaders.org/sister-m-madeleva-wolff/. Accessed October 2023.

Sister Thea Bowman Black Catholic Education Foundation history. (n.d.). Sister Thea Bowman Black Catholic Education Foundation. https://theabowmanfoundation.org/history/. Accessed September 2023.

Sister Thea Bowman's story. (n.d.). Franciscan Sisters of Perpetual Adoration.

https://www.fspa.org/content/about/sister-thea-bowman. Accessed September 2023.

Sommer, Margarete. (n.d.). Yad Vashem: The World Holocaust Remembrance Center. https://righteous.yadvashem.org/?search=margarete%20sommer&searchType=righteous_only&language=en&itemId=4404750&ind=0. Accessed November 2023.

Soskovets, L., S. Krasilnikov and D. Mymrina. (2016). *Persecution of believers as a systemic feature of the Soviet regime*. SHS Web of Conferences , 01098. https://www.shs-conferences.org/articles/shsconf/pdf/2016/06/shsconf_rptss2016_01098.pdf. Accessed March 2024.

Sr. Thea Bowman. (n.d.). Boston College. https://www.bc.edu/content/bc-web/offices/student-affairs/sites/ahana/about/baic-history/sr--thea-bowman.html. Accessed September 2023.

St. Gianna Beretta Molla. (n.d.). Catholic Online. https://www.catholic.org/saints/saint.php?saint_id=6985. Accessed October 2023.

St. Gianna's life. (n.d.). Saint Gianna Beretta Molla. https://saintgianna.org/stgiannalife.htm. Accessed October 2023.

St. Teresa Benedicta of the Cross (Edith Stein). (n.d.). EWTN. https://www.ewtn.com/catholicism/saints/teresa-benedicta-of-the-cross-edith-stein-779. Accessed October 2023.

Sub-Saharan Africa: The Essentials Modern History: Sub-Saharan Africa. (2022, February 8). Council on Foreign Relations. https://education.cfr.org/learn/learning-journey/sub-saharan-africa-essentials/modern-history-sub-saharan-africa. Accessed July 2024.

Surrender of Germany (1945). (n.d.) National Archives. https://www.archives.gov/milestone-documents/surrender-of-germany. Accessed June 2024.

Szanto, S. & Moran, D. (2020). Edith Stein. In *Stanford Encyclopedia of Philosophy*. Retrieved October 9, 2023, from https://plato.stanford.edu/entries/stein/#SteiWorkGerm Engl. Accessed September 2023.

The 1963 March on Washington. (n.d.) NAACP. https://naacp.org/find-resources/history-explained/1963-march-washington. Accessed February 2024.

The History of Commercial Flight: How Global Travel Took Off. (August 13, 2023). Airways. https://airwaysmag.com/how-global-travel-took-off/. Accessed February 2024.

The History of Print from 1900 to 1949. (n.d.). Prepressure. https://www.prepressure.com/printing/history/1900-1949. Accessed March 2024.

The Holocaust. (n.d.). The National WWII Museum. https://www.nationalww2museum.org/war/articles/holocaust. Accessed May 2024.

The Nuremberg Trials. (N.d.) The National World War II Museum. https://www.nationalww2museum.org/war/topics/nuremberg-trials. Accessed May 2024.

The Race for Colonies in Sub-Saharan Africa. (N.d.) Britannica. https://www.britannica.com/topic/Western-colonialism/The-race-for-colonies-in-sub-Saharan-Africa. Accessed July 2024.

Thea Bowman AHANA and intercultural center. (n.d.). Boston College. https://www.bc.edu/bc-web/offices/student-affairs/sites/ahana.html. Accessed October 2023.

Titanic. (January 27, 2024). Britannica. https://www.britannica.com/topic/Titanic. Accessed March 2024.

Titanic. (June 29, 2023). History. https://www.history.com/topics/early-20th-century-us/titanic. Accessed March 2024.

Top 12 Most Deadliest Wars In History. (n.d.). The Borgen
Project. https://borgenproject.org/top-12-deadliest-
wars-in-history/. Accessed March 2024.
Vidal Aguas y Quijano, J. (1987) *The Philippines in the
Twentieth Century: Social Change in Recent The
Philippines in the Twentieth Century: Social Change in
Recent Decades.* College of William & Mary - Arts &
Sciences.
https://scholarworks.wm.edu/cgi/viewcontent.cgi?articl
e=4025&context=etd. Accessed April 2024.
Voigtländer, N., Voth, H. (2015, April 17). *Nazi indoctrination
and anti-Semitic beliefs in Germany.* PNAS.
https://www.pnas.org/doi/full/10.1073/pnas.141482211
2. Accessed June 2024.
Walker, A. & Smith, C. (n.d.). *Thea Bowman.*
https://www.biola.edu/talbot/ce20/database/thea-
bowman. Accessed November 2023.
Wallich, H. (1955). *Mainsprings of the German Revival.* New
Haven: Yale University Press.
Watkins, S. (2013, April 9). *Affirm the fruits of ecumenical
dialogue.* U.S. Catholic.
https://uscatholic.org/articles/201304/affirm-the-fruits-
of-ecumenical-dialogue/. Accessed February 2024.
Way, Y. (2001). *Anuarite Nengapeta.* Dictionary of African
Christian Biography.
https://dacb.org/stories/democratic-republic-of-
congo/anuarite-mc/. Accessed November 2023.
What was Jewish life in Germany like after World War II?
(n.d.). Britannica.
https://www.britannica.com/video/222416/aftereffects-
World-War-II-Germany. Accessed July 2024.
What was the Berlin Wall and how did it fall? (n.d.). Imperial
War Museums. https://www.iwm.org.uk/history/what-
was-the-berlin-wall-and-how-did-it-fall. Accessed June
2024.
Who we are. (n.d.). The Society of the Sisters of Social
Service. https://2021.sssinternational.org/who-we-are/.
Accessed October 2023.

Winters, M.S. (2016, November 1). *Ecumenism in our time: A fruit of the Council.* National Catholic Reporter. https://www.ncronline.org/blogs/distinctly-catholic/ecumenism-our-time-fruit-council. Accessed March 2024.

World War I. (n.d.). History. https://www.history.com/topics/world-war-i/world-war-i-history. Accessed April 2024.

World War II. (n.d.). History. https://www.history.com/topics/world-war-ii. Accessed April 2024.

World War II. (n.d.). Britannica. https://www.britannica.com/place/Italy/End-of-the-regime. Accessed April 2024.

Yellin, D. (2023, September 27). *Can nuns be saved from extinction? Totowa's Little Sisters of the Poor is latest casualty.* northjersey.com. https://www.northjersey.com/story/news/local/2023/09/26/little-sisters-of-the-poor-leave-nj-as-nuns-face-declining-numbers/70437730007/. Accessed June 2024.

Zengarini, L. (2022, October 11). *An Overview of the Second Vatican Council.* Vatican News. https://www.vaticannews.va/en/vatican-city/news/2022-10/vatican-ii-council-60th-anniversary-video-history-background.html. Accessed March 2024.